Advance Praise for
Damsel in Distressed

"This is a witty and wise story of a woman who found success and satisfaction working as an investor in the pointy-end of the finance industry—hedge funds. Dominique tells it all, in a way that entertains and inspires both the veteran investor and the aspiring novice."

— AMANDA PULLINGER, Chief Executive Officer of 100 Women in Finance

"Dominique Mielle tells the story of her hedge fund career with humor and élan, in a way that illuminates both twenty years of hedge fund history and what it took to be one of the few women of her generation to reach the top ranks of finance."

— PROFESSOR JONATHAN LEVIN, Dean of the Stanford Graduate School of Business, Philip H. Knight Professor, Senior Fellow at the Stanford Institute for Economic Policy Research

"Dominique Mielle delivers a witty and inspiring must-read primer on hedge funds. To any woman considering a finance career, and to anyone invested or interested in hedge funds…read this book."

— MARIAM NAFICY, Serial Entrepreneur, Founder and CEO of Minted, Author of *The Fast Track: The Insider's Guide to Winning Jobs in Management Consulting, Investment Banking, & Securities Trading*

"Mielle offers an insider's view of what it's like to be a woman hedge fund manager in an industry overwhelmingly dominated by men. Over a twenty-year career, she describes rising through the ranks to Partner of a $24 billion hedge fund complex with a combination of intelligence, hard work, and an unwillingness to be minimized by genderism."

— SCOTT RICHLAND, Chief Investment Officer of the California Institute of Technology, a $3 billion endowment, Guest Lecturer at Stanford, CalTech, and UCLA

"A funny account of the inner workings of the hedge fund industry from a unique female voice, helpful to both asset management practitioners and aspiring investment professionals."

— SIMON LACK, Author of *The Hedge Fund Mirage*, Founder of SL Advisors and the JPMorgan Incubator

"With her impeccable style, good humor, and an immigrant's common sense, Dominique Mielle treats us to her story—how she made money, and her mark, as one of the country's few women hedge fund investors. A funny, fearless frolic."

— MERIDEE MOORE, Founder and Chief Investment Officer of Watershed Asset Management and Board Member of BlackRock Capital

DAMSEL
IN
DISTRESSED

MY LIFE *in*
the GOLDEN AGE *of*
HEDGE FUNDS

DOMINIQUE MIELLE

Post Hill
PRESS

A POST HILL PRESS BOOK
ISBN: 978-1-64293-972-9
ISBN (eBook): 978-1-64293-973-6

Damsel in Distressed:
My Life in the Golden Age of Hedge Funds
© 2021 by Dominique Mielle
All Rights Reserved

Cover art by Cody Corcoran
Poem permission: U.A. Fanthorpe, Beginner's Luck (Bloodaxe Books, 2019)

Post Hill Press
New York • Nashville
posthillpress.com

Published in the United States of America
1 2 3 4 5 6 7 8 9 10

CONTENTS

It's hard for a girl to be sure if
She wants to be rescued. I mean, I quite
Took to the dragon. It's nice to be
Liked, if you know what I mean.

—U. A. Fanthorpe,
"Not My Best Side"

CHAPTER 1

HAPPY AS A CLOWN

On my first day at Canyon Partners, the Dow Jones dropped 512 points, or more than 6 percent. The Nasdaq had its worst daily loss in history. Bloomberg screens were bleeding and traders fervently wished, a few hours into the session, for a circuit breaker—or their moms. The entire year's gain was neatly wiped out by closing time. Under the circumstances, my entrance may have appeared a touch incongruous, my attitude a tad tone-deaf when I marched into the office that morning, enthusiastic, a spring in my step, deeply tanned from a two-month-long summer vacation after I finished business school. I felt great. Positively delighted to be there. No one warned me that I had arrived amid a financial meltdown. When I interviewed for the position, in April of 1998, the firm managed $1 billion in assets, which seemed both a ludicrously large and pleasantly round number. By the time I started in August of that same year, I overheard that we held $500 million in assets and was quietly perplexed. Had there been a typo in my original notes?

I had not misunderstood. With the capital markets in full-blown crisis mode, the firm had indeed lost half its money in just a few months. The organization had started in 1991 while the hedge fund industry itself was very new, and Canyon debated in its first years whether to be an advisory firm or a hedge fund. The former, like a consulting firm, does not invest capital, whereas the latter focuses on attracting and deploying money from investors. In 1998, along with my arrival as a new employee, came a series of crises of such magnitude that they jeopardized most of the assets, and hence jeopardized the very existence of my new employer.

Asia, particularly Thailand, was engulfed in a currency meltdown that had started the previous summer and threatened to spread to Western economies in a worldwide economic collapse. Russia, meanwhile, was the poster child of overleverage. Its ballooning budget deficit had been financed through debt, a third of which was sold to international investors. As its economy slowed down, the ruble plummeted, inflation ran wild, and interest rates shot up. On August 17, 1998, the country defaulted on its domestic debt, and declared a moratorium on repaying foreign debt. Canyon had invested in Russia, so not only did it lose a good amount of money during the so-called "Russian Flu," but those losses shook investors' confidence to the point that numerous started withdrawing their money.

The biggest hedge fund at the time, Long-Term Capital Management, heavily involved in the Russian treasury bond market and leveraged over twenty times, was hemorrhaging almost $4 billion in losses and facing the unthinkable: bankruptcy. The fund's prospective failure could be so perilous to global financial markets and investors worldwide that it had to forcefully be gobbled up by another hedge fund in a deal hastily arranged by the Federal

Reserve Bank. The head of Long-Term Capital, John Meriwether, had been a legend. The "Bond King," they called him. He was the hero of Michael Lewis's wonderful book *Liar's Poker,* the stuff that every pubescent girl aspiring to be a big deal in finance looks up to.

One could say that Meriwether was caught up in a low-probability, high-consequence sequence of events. Bad luck, in other words. But a lesser-known fact is that Meriwether started two more hedge funds after Long-Term Capital; they both closed too, after seven years or less. It's tough to argue that the man ran out of luck three times in a row.

That is the problem with hedge funds: they are an unstable business model. The remarkable feat about hedge funds is not that managers beat the market consistently (almost none of them do for any extended period)—it is that they last at all. I have calculated that over the past fifteen years, over 9 percent of existing hedge funds closed every year, only to make way for new offspring. As I am writing this book, the hedge fund empires of David Einhorn and Bill Ackman, once the darlings of investors and renowned stock pickers, are under serious pressure. I had my first taste of this in 1998. The market was exploding; a financial crisis had erupted around the world; the biggest and most acclaimed hedge fund in history needed rescuing; and my partners were in shock. I, on the other hand, was happy as a clown—as I believed, in my French confusion, that the saying went. Until an American corrected me: happy as a *clam.*

ON THE BUY-SIDE

I don't mean to sound insensitive. I celebrate no one else's losses, and do not typically mock others—at least not to their faces. I could not restrain myself from feeling mighty satisfied: a Stanford MBA alumna, freshly minted hedge fund analyst, settling in Los Angeles with a Miata convertible! This hubris had no external validation. Most of my acquaintances did not fathom what a hedge fund was, and it was slightly wearisome to have to explain at social gatherings that the hedge part had nothing to do with landscaping. Truthfully, the cool jobs resided in the emerging internet world. It was a time when you had to spell out "www" when citing a website. At an alumni reunion, a few months after graduation in 1998, I sat next to friends who worked, respectively, at eToys, Ecooking, Eve.com and Amazon. The latter was unquestionably bound to fail due to its absurd brand name, as I had helpfully warned the recruiter after declining an interview to become employee number fifteen at the brave little company. "You guys ought to be called eBooks if you want to succeed," I said. Still, I wondered alarmingly over dinner if, years down the road, my kids would judge me. "Did you not *get* what the internet was? Is that why we are poor now?" Then came a reassuring thought: *I didn't want children.*

I was ecstatic about my new employment. After my previous professional experiences, I considered myself ready to be in a position where I could make decisions. I wanted to be judged on what I said, have what I did stand on its own, and be in a place where my work could be evaluated as good or bad, objectively. You are right, you make money; you're wrong, you lose money (which doesn't quite factor in the critical element of luck, but you get my point). The formidable bond investor Jeff Gundlach calls it the "bloodless verdict of the markets." It is a score, and I wanted to win. I did not want to be in a corporation so large that what I thought mattered only marginally, and to stay there so long that I got lost. I wanted to make a difference.

My previous longest employment, as an investment banker at Lehman Brothers in New York and then Los Angeles, was the diametric opposite of that. I spent most waking hours working on slide presentations handed down by the associate, who reported to the vice president, who heard the pitch from the managing director. By the time it got to me, the message was as diluted as a bloody Mary on American Airlines. At the time, we analysts drew each slide on paper and handed the sheet over to the image processing department, the sole and holy repository of PowerPoint software, graphic computers, and color printers (we reigned over Lotus 1-2-3—which, note to the millennial reader—was not a meditation app). Imagine an immense call center staffed 24/7, but with people transcribing the doodling and bullet points of hundreds of bankers in their heroic yet verbose effort to sell a stock, a bond, a merger transaction—you name it—to a corporate board of directors. A single slide could take hours, and each was slotted in the queue with thousands other slides; it had to be picked up by a designer, processed, and returned to you to proofread. Alas, these aspiring artists took the most wonderfully nonchalant liberties with our designs. Charts lost their legends, graphs their proportion, logos their color, and bullet points their spelling. I had to review, correct, and resubmit—and so it went, again and again, a miserable Groundhog Day for a twenty-page presentation. In the wee hours of the morning, I once read the daring but perhaps true statement "A high-call premium can become an incontinence." I did almost wet myself laughing, but the inconvenience was all mine to get the typo fixed. In the end, after an all-nighter, the spiral-bound finished product solemnly handed over to the senior banker, you could be dumbfounded by a pronouncement such as "I don't like Cambria 13 font." I don't like pompous prats myself, but there we were, weren't we? On the bright side, no brainpower was exerted, no intellectual energy utilized, no mental capacity required in this line of work. It was just a game of brute-force face time bordering on the absurd. Of course, the occasional interesting deal and meeting would occur; these were mostly a blur in the life of a processing automaton.

I lasted, under varying degrees of despondency, almost three years. It is deeply miserable to routinely work over a hundred hours a week with no end in sight. It takes a toll. I swear I worked with a very genial vice president who, faced with the unusual situation of introducing me to his family at a company event, had forgotten the name of his own children. There was a name for the routine that consisted of calming down the rage that would finally drive a spouse to show up at Three World Trade Center on a Saturday night at 10:45, demanding an immediate explanation for why they had waited two hours at the restaurant: "the walk-and-talk." Quite literally, the banker would come down sixteen floors and walk around the atrium, explaining and apologizing until, the situation diffused, it was time to go right back up to work. "Jamie Dimon? Back in a jiffy. He's doing the walk-and-talk with his wife." I do not know if the new offices' architects got clued in on incorporating a walking track of sorts, but it was a must-have design back in the days.

One young woman who started after me projected a mirror of what I might become. She was a cute, sharp girl in her twenties, fresh out of college. By the end of three months, the demands of the job had overcome her ability to do laundry and her stockings had gaping holes. After six months, her hygiene had become suspicious, even by my French standards. We might climb our way up to associate or vice president, but then we would just have to work as much or more—and we would smell like hell. Since my ambition closely cohabits with my considerable vanity, I worried.

The managing director I reported to at Lehman in Los Angeles properly defined brutal workaholism. Fittingly, he had a vague resemblance to the actor Ed Harris, who so masterfully played Jackson Pollock, another guy with compulsive behavior—clearly a superior genius at throwing paint around but, in fairness to my old boss, probably inept at picking lovely bullet points. He spent his life in the office and doggedly committed his team to do so as well.

The lone weekend I was able to escape to go skiing in Big Bear, he called me back on Sunday morning and I finished the weekend sweating profusely through my leggings and ski pants in the office, which had no air conditioning outside of business hours.

I worked for him during the Northridge earthquake of 1994. He managed to get to the office through the fractured freeway, triumphally ascended thirteen floors without an elevator or electricity, and phoned me at home.

"We're going to meet at my house and work tonight," he announced, all gleeful.

"What about the curfew?" I asked, concerned that the mayor had issued a state of emergency. My boss's opinion was that it was optional; that's when I knew the job was not for me. Call me particular, but I had no interest in going around breaking the law to get a merger done. With all due respect to my boss's intellectual power and his physical prowess, I didn't want to be paid a fee to run analytics that helped other people make a decision, not on a night when local authorities bound me to stay home, nor on any other. In retrospect, I should have known what I was in for when an associate had me work through the night from a hotel room in downtown Manhattan after we were dislodged from the Lehman office by the first World Trade Center bombing in 1993. It is not exactly that I am slow; rather, persistence and stubbornness are difficult for me to distinguish.

In the end, for all the hours you put in, you are not on the line in corporate finance, not *really*. It is a service business where, while you do make decisions, they are consulting decisions with no investment risk. Undoubtedly, it was excellent training; I learned a lot even as a lowly analyst. However, modeling scenarios of a company issuing bonds or stocks or analyzing mergers and acquisitions give you surprisingly little clue about investing. You're never truly evaluating what the company is worth, if the bonds are good value, whether the stock is attractive, or what you would change in the business or restructure in the capital if you could, because you simply don't have money at stake. You try to get things processed and packaged in a neat little pitch book that proves your worth to a senior banker and ultimately to the client. It seemed a lot of work for little credit and even less ownership.

By the end of three years at Lehman, I knew it was time to move on. I needed a break from workaholism, a change in professional direction, and some good times. I applied to business school.

SHARP FOCUS

I became interested in the buy-side (the business that consists of buying financial securities, as opposed to the sell-side, which sells them) during my MBA studies at Stanford. Two courses were true revelations because of their intellectual content and the motivation they provided to look for an investment job. Both were mixed PhD and MBA classes, which, to me, gave them immediate credibility. I will freely admit that I am a sucker for education titles, and PhD screams of respectability. The courses required a lot of math, which I had a strong background in. The educational system in France is very math-heavy, and the path to a good degree at a prestigious university goes through math, or at least it did back in my days. My father is gifted in math; my brother is gifted in math. I was a lot less talented but a lot more hardworking, so I made up for any of my deficiencies through brute force.

The first was a class in risk management taught by Darrell Duffie. Professor Duffie was instrumental in my conviction that risk tolerance is a skill, like financial analysis or bankruptcy reorganization, that you learn and refine. It is a muscle that you exercise and stretch. Risk tolerance is no different from physical endurance. Everyone has some; it's only a matter of degree. What matters is how you quantify and manage it, or in finance terms, the amount of return you garner per unit of risk, a concept aptly named the Sharpe ratio, conceived by the 1990 Nobel laureate in economic sciences, William F. Sharpe.

Which brings me to the other class that remains seared in my mind. Simply called portfolio management, it was taught by Bill Sharpe himself, a pioneer in financial economics, whose Capital Asset Pricing Model revolutionized portfolio management theory. I had a hopeless crush on him, though he was already in his sixties then and somewhat heavyset—not to mention married. I sat in the front of the class. I raised my hand. I told other students to shut up if they made noise, even opening their books. I volunteered to do the group homework. The Stanford administrative staff had innocently cooked up a program called Invite Your Professor to Lunch, so I dutifully invited him to a meal on campus, supposedly to discuss a thesis on currency correlation, which I never wrote the first sentence of and haven't given another thought to until just now. No, if Professor Sharpe ever reads this, I'll have to come clean that I was barely listening to what he was saying I was so enraptured. He ordered a bacon and avocado burger. Little bits and pieces stuck to his beard. *How cute,* I thought. I am an incurable romantic.

I traveled back to Stanford recently to be a guest speaker for two back-to-back finance classes. The topic was the conflict of interest between bondholders and stockholders. The material seemed very technical in nature. Essentially, stockholders own a call option on the value of a company while bondholders have sold a put option. One constituent is long volatility while the other is short—they are consequently at odds in times of changing volatility. In both classes, however, a female student asked about how hard it was to manage these conflicts in a hedge fund job. Meaning, how to deal with clashes on a personal level.

I am used to all kinds of questions. Once, after what I considered a rather eloquent public speech on investing in aviation in the post-9/11 era, I was approached by a woman. "I have a question," she said a bit sheepishly. Thinking she had been too shy to raise her hand in the audience, I encouraged her with a reassuring nod, so she continued. "Where did you buy these fabulous boots?"

Nevertheless, I was taken aback by what was being asked in the Stanford classroom. Isn't life full of battles and tough decisions, big and small, personal and professional, that each of us handles in his or her own way? Trading conflicts are no different. Different investors have distinctive styles, probably reflecting how they deal with conflicts everywhere—some yell, some threaten, some negotiate, some outsmart, some charm. It should certainly not scare away anyone, women included, from trying their hand at the job.

It isn't lost on me that this is one of the reasons why women in finance, and specifically women in hedge funds, are so underrepresented. Forceful decision-making, particularly if portrayed as a brash, aggressive, in-your-face behavior, as Wall Street is commonly pictured, is not necessarily taught to or embraced by women. It may not reflect a skill that they like or want to identify with. Men generally don't believe being assertive is a feminine aptitude.

But there is no conflict between being decisive and being nice; perhaps that is the essence of what my female interlocutors wanted to be reassured of during my recent Stanford appearances. You don't have to take a job where you can be nice. You can be nice in the job you take. And you should be. I have seen my share of aggressive hedge fund analysts in management meetings, exclusively men (primarily young and inexperienced ones), often wearing khaki pants that are too short and an outdoor vest best designed for camping, be abrasive and forceful in their questions. Guess what? They do not get answers. Who wants to help those thugs? Being nonconfrontational, approachable, and relatable is an enormous advantage when you meet the management of a company to get a good sense for their business. You might occasionally get a straight response on Wall Street.

There are studies that seem to conclude that women are more risk averse than men. But it does not follow that men are better decision makers or investors. Some people, Evel Knievel for example, thrive at risk-taking. Knievel was the stuntman who successfully launched his motorcycle 133 feet over fourteen Greyhound buses, but that would not necessarily make him a good hedge fund manager—just a good candidate for groin injury. In fact, one study shows that men tend to overtrade, thereby reducing their net risk-adjusted returns by 2.6 percent.[1] Good investors do not relish risk for the sake of it. Rather, they tolerate risk. They can endure being proven wrong, and all the garden-variety unpleasantness that comes with it: being judged and mocked by your colleagues (somehow news of a losing investment always gets around faster than a winning one); being yelled at by the partners; and, generally speaking, looking like an imbecile for what feels like an extended period of time. And yet, a determined investor, whether male or female, still shows up the next day as if nothing happened. Or rather, as if he or she has lost money and must make it up, which means working harder to recoup the loss.

GUESSING GAME

I had tried my hand at investing the summer before joining Canyon, as an intern in an equity mutual fund. They parked me in a closet and asked me to research ideas. I kid you not, my shoes at home take up more space than I did in this office. The firm had a somewhat formulaic research process, applying screening criteria to a list of companies from a printout thicker than the *Encyclopedia Britannica*. My job was to calculate ratios from the companies' financial statements and check them against the hurdles. It went more or less like this: pass, it's a buy; fail, it's a sell. I did not experience such a level of tediousness again until years later, when I breastfed my firstborn every hour and a half, ten times a day. For some it is a bonding experience; it just was not my thing. And—to the one attentive and finicky reader wondering, *Wait, didn't she just write she didn't want children?*—that is correct; life is not linear. I don't do long-term personal forecasting. I have no overarching motto, unyielding principle, or specific endpoint. John Lennon sang that life is what happens to you when you're busy making other plans in "Beautiful Boy." I have two myself. But my husband once cunningly observed that, had Chanel launched a maternity fashion line, I may have had another.

I digress. Back to Canyon. The opportunity to make a wide range of creative decisions in ever-changing markets and investments is the reason I was so excited to join this Los Angeles-based hedge fund, then mostly dedicated to special situations and distressed investments. In addition, they enjoyed a pedigree of the noblest level in my ranking, the founders being former close associates of Michael Milken, the financial guru creator of the junk bond market at the now-defunct investment bank Drexel Burnham Lambert. When I met the founders for my interview, I was wearing five-inch stilettos, making me five feet nine, which, by the way, is rather tall in the world of high finance. One partner was coming from the gym. They were all wearing jeans or sweats while I was done up in a proper suit and a briefcase. It probably looked like the *Working Girl* (I am referring to the movie with Melanie Griffith, not the euphemism) had resurrected from the '80s. One of them grinned and asked, "Did you dress up for us?"

On my first day, I settled at a desk in an open space the size of a large conference room, which was the entire footprint of Canyon. The trading floor had only one trader and one assistant. There were a handful of shared offices, and these were reserved for the founding partners and a couple of senior analysts. The rest of us, about a dozen people in total including the trader and back-office staff, were crammed onto the open floor. You could hear everybody's conversations. There were no cell phones at the time, hence no way to step out and make a personal call. If I had to call the beauty salon for an emergency bikini-wax appointment (who doesn't?), or if (and I don't wish to imply this is a true story) a car dealer called a senior colleague to deliver the 911 Porsche that his wife had unbeknownst to him bought herself with his year-end bonus, it was awkward. The close quarters gave Canyon a congenial atmosphere, but it was a high-pressure firm—sink or swim. It was entrepreneurial. There was no one to train me. They could not take manpower to divert it into some extensive coaching program even if they wished to. They simply did not have it. The firm was too small. They wanted people who could figure it out on their own. I had received the 1998 prize in the Stanford Entrepreneurship Challenge (we were going to set up a software company to value esoteric interest rate options, but my PhD partners disappeared with the award money), yet the truth is this: I had no clue about investing. I really didn't know a thing. But for the first time, I envisioned a career. I foresaw a grand adventure. And I was determined to make the most of it.

Week one, the partner gave me a position to analyze. "Why don't you take a look at Nextel?" he said. We stood at the infancy of the wireless industry, which promised to become an exciting new field of investments. In 1993, there were only thirty-four million wireless subscribers, or 13 percent of the U.S. population— imagine, less than one in seven people had a cell phone! Nextel was a revolutionary company, one of the first operators to offer a portable, wireless handset. In truth, Nextel technology back then worked more like a walkie-talkie than a cell phone, using radio frequencies usually designated for fleet dispatch (in fact, Nextel was called FleetCall before changing its name in 1993). But it claimed many firsts—first to offer cellular coverage nationwide, first to offer unlimited calling plans, first to offer GPS on their phones, and first to upgrade their network to 2G. I did not own a cell phone and knew nothing of the company, except that this could become my *first* trade! *I got this*, I thought with a grin.

He directed me to listen to the conference call at 5:30 in the morning announcing the company's earnings—that's what you get when you work in Los Angeles, while financial news is released three thousand miles to the east and three hours earlier. I dialed in from my bed. Naive mistake. In the middle of the presentation, I fell into the luxurious slumber of those innocents who do not have a position to trade or a portfolio to manage. Not only was it indecently early in the morning, but the lingo was also reprehensible. ARPU (average revenue per user), churn (average percentage of customer defection), and SAC (subscriber acquisition cost) were some of the terms confidently thrown around by the management team, as if everyone on the call knew what they meant. And they probably did—except me. When I arrived in the office, the partner asked how many subscribers the company had signed up in the quarter. I blanked. "A million," I ventured with gusto. Then, reading his incredulity, "A hundred," I conceded. His face still didn't look right. "Alright, a thousand, maybe?" I offered conciliatorily. I had no idea. "Does it start with a B? What does it rhyme with?" No, I didn't ask that. This wasn't bingo. I never dared improvising an answer again. I did, however (and this is a testimony to my partner's indulgence), continue to follow Nextel on and off for the next decades. Companies have a funny way of going through phases, much like people. They grow, they mature, they partner up in a merger, they fail and re-emerge, and they age with various degrees of grace. Each phase provides an opportunity for trades and profits under different investment strategies. In Nextel's case, those phases included high-yield bonds as the company financed its growth, risk arbitrage when it merged with Sprint, and distressed investing as Nextel International, which was divested in the acquisition, filed for bankruptcy…twice, and was finally sold in pieces. Building knowledge of a company and understanding its life cycles brings an immense competitive advantage to an investor. It allows you to react quicker, forecast better, analyze deeper.

That's the theory anyway. For me, the first trade was undeniably an inauspicious beginning.

CHAPTER 2

THE EARLY DAYS

If you have ever read about hedge fund investors, you will know that the calling from above to enter the order of Wall Street comes early. Ray Dalio, the billionaire investor behind Bridgewater Associates, the largest hedge fund in the world today, began investing at twelve, buying shares in Northeast Airlines and tripling his money when the company was bought. Ken Griffin, the founder of Citadel, a $32 billion global investment firm, started his first fund in college at Harvard. Steve Cohen, the famed billionaire who created SAC Capital and now owns the New York Mets, started trading while a student at Wharton. Paul Tudor Jones started trading commodities right after college, declining to attend Harvard Business School to pursue his love of investing. In short, if you failed to capitalize on (or did your poor soul fail to even recognize it?) the arbitrage opportunity between the price of lemon and sugar and that of lemonade as a child, why really, what contribution could you possibly make to the great world of finance wizardry?

THE GRAPES OF WEALTH

I had never read a hedge fund book, nor, come to think of it, any finance book other than *Liar's Poker* and classroom textbooks until I started writing my own, and then I decided to check out the competition. There are excellent, nuanced, and well-researched nonfictions, including my favorites, *When Genius Failed* and *Black Edge*, the latter written, as luck would have it, by a female journalist. I have observed, however, from my casual perusing of biographies, that most of my esteemed male colleagues in finance appear to be—how shall I put it?—gods. They may have started from simple means, but these paragons of self-drive fought herculean obstacles. They followed the divine call to enter the stock market. They developed mythical foresight while building imperial fortunes, all in the span of some forty-odd years. And for the modest sum of $13.99 or so, and I must say here that I find the extra ninety-nine cents reprehensible in view of the authors' net worth of some $20 billion, I too could be imparted with the wisdom of their *Principles*, their *Lessons in the Pursuit of Excellence,* and, don't mind if I do, *Earn [my] First Billion Dollars*. When the book is not autobiographical, the lionization subsists or expands, unbridled. The inescapable conclusion is that we simply cannot have enough tomes deifying the hedge fund alpha male.

By the way, in the categories of literature I dislike, let me hasten to lump in the how-to and self-help genres, which many hedge fund books fall under. These books expose inadequacies that I had no idea existed, let alone limited my ability to be effective, make friends, and enjoy the power of now. I don't randomly *Lean In* or routinely *Bite the Ass Off a Bear*, I can't follow seven habits, much less thirteen principles, in business or otherwise. I digress, but a well-intentioned friend once gave me a book about putting your child to sleep after I casually mentioned, and this was small talk you understand, that my firstborn turned into a poltergeist around bedtime. *Baby Wise* or *Baby Whisperer* or something similarly aspirational was the title. By the time I finished the second chapter, I resolved to have a second child immediately, seeing that I had botched everything and irremediably ruined my first. I never read a self-help book again. The upshot is that I do not like to be told what to do; I like being told how to do it even less.

Back to the topic of investing. Unlike some of the mythical origin tales of my male counterparts, my calling was late and weak. A hedge fund murmur at best. How did they miss *me* in the hedge fund pantheon when they issued such clear divine vocational orders to so many others? Incomprehensible, really, considering the facts.

I attended the most prestigious business university (HEC Paris), a venerable institution founded in 1881 that produced most French CEOs, including the leaders of Danone, L'Oréal, Michelin, and—if you exclude former president and alumnus François Hollande—a number of very capable politicians. For the neophytes in French politics, Hollande is the only president in the Fifth Republic, established over sixty years ago, not to seek re-election because his popularity was so low. He ran his 2012 presidential political campaign against his former partner and the mother of his four children, Ségolène Royal, which is strange even by the standards of *Days of Our Lives*, then settled down with his girlfriend and first lady at the Elysée Palace only to be photographed on a scooter, zooming to a secret rendezvous with his new actress lover, by paparazzi. This being France, his approval rate went up two points after the exposé but still stayed in the teens, making him the most unpopular president in modern history.

Granted, all this might be a tad obscure for a non-French reader, but how about Salma Hayek? I bet you know *her*. Well, she most definitely did not study business management at HEC. Her billionaire husband, Francois Henri Pinault, owner of such luxury brands as Gucci, Yves Saint Laurent, and Balenciaga, did.

The education system is similar to that of the U.S. only in the fact that although there is a plethora of universities for each curriculum, they greatly vary in prestige, which itself is largely driven by how low the acceptance rate is. HEC is the French equivalent of Princeton or Cambridge. The admission process was a cruel selection that started with a year of what can only be described as forced labor studies in topics ranging from philosophy and literature, history, geography, and political science to foreign languages (two are required) and loads of math. It's called *classe préparatoire*, and no foreigner would ever imagine such a cute and preppy name stands for sheer misery and Everest levels of stress, culminating in written exams, followed by (only if you pass the writing) oral exams. The oral exam is public, in front of a jury. Imagine presenting the properties of matrix multiplication or debating why the first Soviet five-year plan led to famine—in front of an unruly crowd. Family members, friends, and professors were encouraged to show up and root for their candidate, which didn't so much mean silently supporting them as hissing, laughing, interrupting, or otherwise disrupting the presentations of competing applicants. A final score was tallied after the oral test and every student ranked accordingly. The first two hundred were accepted; the other five to ten thousand applicants were rejected. One could only attempt the entrance exams twice in a lifetime. When I saw the movie *Gladiator*, years later, I realized that Russell Crowe had done method acting with an alumnus from my alma matter.

I failed the first year. I did not even make it to the oral exam. I spent the summer either crying, in a state of regressive stupor, or following my mother around like a puppy. A month of her nineteen-year-old daughter pushing the supermarket cart in tears led her to inquire if I was sure that HEC was the right spot. There were many other less demanding—and less prominent—schools to which I could apply the next year, which would undoubtedly accept me. To propose an option that lessened the pressure and lowered the bar was unlike her. She had high expectations—and so did I, which is why I felt so broken.

My mother was a steadfast supporter of mine, which is not to say she wasn't discerning. As a girl, I heard her declare more than once that I was not exactly pretty or cute, but more "interesting-looking." But she had no doubts about my intellect. This she observed analytically and with great love, in the scientific spirit of helping me use my best attribute, my brain, rather than my face. I received and classified the information as such, a helpful pointer to a winning horse. It made academic failure even more searing. However, as I mentioned, persistence and stubbornness are very blurry in my personality, whereas my ego is so sharply defined that I am almost surprised there isn't a neon sign pointing to me, flashing "Caution! Type A Personality Crossing!" It's my strength and my cross.

I don't mean the latter in that I was the victim of a bias against female power or competitiveness—at least not in France and not back then. The double standard undoubtedly exists on this side of the pond. In a survey done in 2019, the Pew Research Center found that Americans are much more likely to use the words "powerful," "leadership," and "ambition" in a positive way to describe men (60 percent to 92 percent positive) than women (75 percent to 92 percent negative). On the contrary, my parents embraced my ambition, which they considered a virtue, and stoically accepted as part of the package the impatience, bad temper, obsessiveness, and other control-freakishness that came along. These side effects can be a liability. I read that type A people are more likely to suffer from coronary disease, but then again, most of us run eight miles a day; follow a strict nonfat, low-sugar diet; drink only occasionally; floss three times a day; and meditate thirty minutes every morning.

So it was that the following school year, I set out to work like a dog and simultaneously predicted that I would most certainly fail again but die trying. I don't wish to sound contradictory; I just am. Trying my hardest while predicting the worst outcome is a balanced state for me. In that precise frame of mind, I resolved to try again.

The second time around, I made it through the writing stage. The week of the oral tests could have been the rehearsal for a bad pregnancy if I did not have such a robust farmland constitution, as I threw up every morning before the exam. I was accepted that year with a score that put me at the top end of the class. I remember my ranking (OK, number seven out of two hundred admitted if you *must* snatch it out of me) because my mother spent her life advertising it to her family and friends, her dentist, hairdresser, oncologist, my boyfriends, and in-laws (despite not speaking the same language). She found new ways, or resorted to old ones, to shamelessly brag.

VOLTAIRE VERSUS VANDERBILT

The funny twist about my university is that after being recruited through a liberal arts prism, students were expected to follow, or even more shockingly, enjoy an almost exclusively business-related coursework, barring a few electives. It was akin to plucking Voltaire from his richly intellectual century (aka the Enlightenment) and plunging him into Wall Street on the first day of school. Not that I fancied myself a modern Voltaire, of course, but if I had to pick, the man seemed eminently more worthy of emulation than John Rockefeller or Cornelius Vanderbilt.

At the time, my interests were pure and theoretical. I had a vague idea that I would need a profession somewhere down the road but held a quiet hope that that road would be long and winding.

I had never worked and was in no hurry to start. Management and business classes seemed tedious; I lived for the electives. I remember exactly three classes from my two years at HEC.

Freud and the Study of Neurosis was a wonderful complement to my enthusiastic read of Freud's oeuvre, particularly *The Interpretation of Dreams* and *Psychopathology of Everyday Life.* I wrote a dissertation on the topic of the housewife psychosis (the obsessional and compulsive cleaning mentioned by one of Freud's patients, Ida Bauer), which as it turns out, my teenage sons believe I suffer from. Italian Art History rekindled my love of Renaissance and Baroque paintings at a time when I had strayed toward more modern periods. And the Japanese language class proved a whimsical brainteaser as it was an elective and I didn't really have to get anywhere with it.

On the other hand, I hated and almost flunked finance. Accounting seemed as useful as crocheting and about as engrossing as basket weaving. I figured myself headed for a marketing job at Procter & Gamble because picking the color of a toothpaste package seemed less tedious. Truthfully, I didn't much care about what job I got back then, so long as it allowed me to move out of Paris, preferably somewhere exotic, warm, and beachy. I tried my hands at various enlightening internships over the school summers, including a three-month stint at the state-owned electric utility in Guadeloupe, West Indies, where my job was to conduct focus groups among linemen and foremen to improve client relationships and productivity. It took a bit of time for these tough-looking, Creole-speaking, heavily unionized folks to warm up to my irresistible incompetence. My service to the good ratepayers of Guadeloupe was nothing if not significant, and it most definitely was not significant, but I sure enjoyed the beach and have a sweet memory of a professional sailboat skipper. I worked in Singapore for a quarter, doing some menial secretarial tasks that I can no more recall than the company I worked for. I do vividly remember water skiing, eating chili crab, and traveling all over Indonesia. I went on a six-week immersion program in Tokyo, with language classes in the morning and corporate visits in the afternoon. Japanese culture held—it still does—a special place in my heart. I had a strong interest in Kabuki and Noh theater, was an avid reader of Mishima and a devoted spectator of Kurosawa. Above all, I loved woodblock prints from the Edo period, also known as "pictures from a floating world."

It was so seductively foreign to a pimply twenty-two-year old. There is no denying it, I had acne until late in life. In Japan, it blossomed much like the cherries. I became acutely self-conscious, particularly in an unfamiliar but loving household with customs that my language lessons had not prepared me for. The family who welcomed me was unusual in that it consisted of a working single mother and her daughter. The husband had died many years before, leaving his wife to run the family business. They were strong-willed women, warm and funny, eager to make me feel comfortable in their home in an upper-class suburb of Tokyo. They kindly tolerated my need to be treated like a young child in everyday life. I was unaware, for example, that one takes a shower *before* entering the bathtub so that one is clean and need not empty the tub water thereafter. My Japanese being still approximate, or perhaps I just appeared a bit slow on the uptake, my host mother made sure of the proper protocol by frequently barging into the bathroom and educating me, butt naked and shivering with cold and embarrassment, in the art of bathing.

The business encounters in the afternoon brought a completely different set of feelings: shock and outrage. It was my first encounter with what I perceived as inequality at work. The only women we met in the program wore uniforms and served tea. Men did neither. It enraged me. It was all the more upsetting that I came home at night to a female CEO. I brought it up in several meetings, and the most frequent explanation—or perhaps the only one that I could understand in Japanese—that women wear nicer clothes, hence the protection of a uniform to serve tea that could splash and stain—left me dumbfounded. Angry. Not to put too fine a point on it, but it wasn't so much the sexism that annoyed me as the existence of a harebrained rule about dress code. I dislike rules; it's a principle. I may even venture to say that I dislike authority and discipline. Call me French, but I find rules generally constraining if not deplorable when they apply to me. I hold a surprisingly more lenient view toward rules for others.

My father takes the medal for disliking rules and being told what to do, almost regardless of the price to pay. He graduated from the top engineering school in France, the equivalent of MIT, the first in his family to go to college. It was the '50s. The pro-independence sentiment in Algeria, the oldest and allegedly most important French colony, solidified into the creation of the National Liberation Army and quickly escalated into a brutal, ruthless, guerilla-style war. Military service was mandatory for one year for all French men. Conscription had existed in France since the Revolution, and the Algerian war made extensive use of draftees from metropolitan France. My twenty-something-year-old father, on account of his education, was virtually assured of a cushy office job away from the calamity zones. Indeed, his school was one of six to impose military instruction on its students during the three-year term, in return for which they obtained a higher grade than soldier. And although they were to serve a year, in accordance with the mandatory military service, only half was spent on the ground and the rest in the office of a military administration. All it took was to perform decently at the military exam, which determined an officer's ranking, and his ability to choose an army corps. But my father deemed the military drills intolerably dim-witted.

Disassembling and cleaning a gun, why, that was dumb but he begrudgingly complied. Target-shooting exercises? He considered the target, and then genially punched holes in place of bullets in the cardboard silhouette with a ballpoint pen. I chortled along with him the first time he told me the story, until he added, "I got caught. I was absolute last in the military exam." He was therefore duly shipped to Algeria for two years, a lieutenant leading a forty-soldier *harka* on the ground, to fight a war on principles he rather opposed against a people he quite sympathized with. He is a highly reserved person, and I never dared ask but I sense it was terrible. He still thinks it's funny, though, in a "I-really-showed-them-didn't-I" kind of way, and far be it from me to ask precisely who showed whom what.

REASONABLE BEYOND DOUBT

My internship experiences abroad inspired me to find a full-time job in Tahiti. If you fail to see a logical thread, it is because there was none. I truly lacked professional drive for a job that wouldn't ship me somewhere fun. Don't judge harshly. A Tahiti gig was no easy goal given that I was in Paris, had never set foot in Tahiti, and considering that the major industries in Tahiti are coconut and sandalwood oil refining, fishing, screen printing, and tourism. What I knew of this tropical paradise came entirely from Paul Gauguin, the nineteenth-century Impressionist painter who had rendered an idyllic image of island life with scenes of languorous native women in colorful garb. Armed with this rather superficial information, I focused my sizeable energy and motivation on starting a professional life in French Polynesia. The opportunity came in the form of a loophole in a French army regulation. As I explained, conscription required all young men to perform at least a year of military service or, for those with higher education, an eighteen-month internship with an embassy, a consulate, or another form of government office in overseas French territories. And there it was one day, on the school job board, a posting by the tourist office of Papeete, Tahiti, advertising an opening for a draftee.

No one said women could not volunteer for the military draft. So I did. After several rounds of interviews, I met the ultimate authority figure at the Ministry of Defense. A stately general in full costume, he evidently had rehearsed and regurgitated the same speech to many generations of young male soldiers, because he warned me thusly: "Do not think the army is sending you to Tahiti to frolic with young girls and pursue a year of debauchery and indiscipline. We will not tolerate any kind of sexual misconduct from our recruits." I solemnly swore. Did I have any questions for him? he asked. Only one, I said. Could he kindly confirm my understanding that, should I be rejected for this job, I would be relieved from duty rather than required to pick up a rifle and join a military command? His answer terrified me; he did not know. And I never found out because I got the job. I was to work in marketing for the Tahiti Chamber of Commerce for a period of only eighteen months with no chance of a permanent position. I imagined it entailed creative administrative tasks along the lines of alphabetically ordering the members' files (or should it be by industry?), organizing the coconut-carving enterprise's monthly get-together, or setting up conferences on topics such as screen printing versus tie dye—which way forward? It was the sort of professional dead end that could perhaps not exactly raise concerns about your mental state, but definitely cause any headhunter with a shred of common sense to question your integrity and work ethic. That was my top choice—that is, until my parents questioned my mental state. They did not tell me what to do because, and here is the annoying part about my parents, they almost never did. They just pondered aloud. And so it was that I also applied, as a backup, for a credit analyst job in New York with one of the largest French banks at the time, Crédit Lyonnais. The position, a one-year trial period with a potential full-time offer back in the Paris office, was part of a well-established program designed by the bank to attract high-achieving students to the field of finance, particularly risk management, trading, and proprietary investing. It wasn't Tahiti, Gauguin, and pearl fishing, but it was overseas, it sounded legit, and I reluctantly pegged myself as a reasonable person. In September 1991, I signed up with a heavy heart, dispirited, forlorn, and boarded a plane. Destination: Wall Street.

How did I leave my native country, my comfortable studio, my family, boyfriend, and friends to start a professional life in the U.S., where I had no one, in an industry that I knew nothing of, and in a city still reeling from the recession initiated by the 1987 Wall Street crash? Few remember that between 1987 and 1991, the median home price in Manhattan had dropped by more than a quarter, the city lost a tenth of its jobs, and the streets were lined with homeless people and drug addicts, many of whom suffered from acute mental conditions. In other words, it was a rough town.

I did not want to spend my entire life in Paris. Therefore, the logical conclusion was that I should not spend another year there after graduating from HEC. I have only foggy memories of how it felt to get on a plane and move to a strange place. It was action-driven rather than emotion-filled—finding a roommate, renting an apartment, meeting my work colleagues, and understanding the job, rather than feeling homesick, anxious, and scared.

I recently heard a podcast with Jim Koch, the cofounder of Boston Beer Company, brewer of Samuel Adams beer. He has an interesting view about risk-taking. Specifically, he highlighted the difference between something scary and something dangerous. Rappelling from a boulder into the void feetfirst is scary but not dangerous, he said, because you're securely tied to a rope that could hold the weight of a car. However, walking across a soft snow patch in a canyon on a sunny and warm spring afternoon is not scary, but it's dangerous because that's the most likely time and place for an avalanche. I could relate, as I am a longtime skier and joyfully endure hours of backcountry hiking in the hope of some elusive virgin powder. He proceeded to relate this concept to his leaving a job at the Boston Consulting Group to start a small artisan brewery. It was scary to quit but not dangerous, because "the real risk," he said, "is wasting your life and not doing what you really want to do." Again, I nodded and enthusiastically cheered in approval.

I often look like a lunatic in my car because I either pretend to conduct a symphony with my music playlist or carry on a lively debate with a podcast. Now, let's not be dramatic or disingenuous here. Jim Koch, a white man in his professional prime (mid-thirties), a JD-MBA graduate from the Harvard Business School, left a six-figure-paying, first-class-flying, corner-office job at a leading consulting firm to begin a brewing company, a business that three generations of Koch men had been involved with, which he started with a secret beer recipe from his family. Both options were excellent, and most people cannot count on a head start from their father, or the fallback of a dual Ivy League degree and a consulting career, should their venture fail. But Mr. Koch made a judicious choice, judging by the phenomenal success of his enterprise, and his point remains that the real risk in life is to have regrets. If you can, pursue self-fulfillment rather than comfort, conventions, and norms. That was my choice.

The year was 1991. Leon Cooperman founded Omega Advisors. Ken Griffin had established Citadel a year earlier with $4.6 million. Steve Cohen started SAC Capital with $10 million in 1992. David Tepper created Appaloosa Management the year after with $57 million. One more thing: in 1991, Canyon Capital launched its first fund. It was the infancy, year zero of the modern hedge fund history. The investing legends, the masters of the universe, the titans of Wall Street, were getting on their way.

I knew absolutely nothing of them.

CHAPTER 3

EMBRACING OTHERNESS

Canyon took a chance in hiring me, for which I was—no, for which I am—perennially grateful. I was not a complete wild guess without any relevant credentials. I had tangentially related competence—a business degree and a background in banking—and I came with excellent professional recommendations, including from ex-Drexel associates close to the Canyon founding partners. But I had no experience on the buy-side and no extensive network on Wall Street, nor among high-net-worth investors. In addition, I am French, which is to say, relative to the average hedge fund comrade, a raging Socialist—a fact that likely did not come to light until later in my career. Most of all, there is the surefire fact that I am a woman. In other words, not exactly a hedge fund catch, except in my mother's mind (she never doubted that any corporation would be lucky to have me in any capacity). Somehow, we jelled.

At the time, as is largely true today some twenty years later, there were no women anywhere in the business, except for the assistants. The secretary to the partners was a woman, as was the assistant trader and the assistant controller. However, the front office—the investment team—was a female-free zone, as on every other hedge fund and most banks' trading floors. I did not take notice at the time; everything was so new that I'm not sure I would have objected to working with Teletubbies.

There were no minorities either. The first time I remember seeing an African American in the office was one early morning around 2007. An imposing, handsome man with a killer smile was pouring himself a cup of coffee in the common kitchen. I said hello.

"Did you see him?" asked another analyst, visibly excited, when I returned to my desk.

"Yes," I enthusiastically confirmed, "I think it's fabulous to bring diversity to the team."

"What are you talking about?" he responded. "That was Magic Johnson. He is heading the Canyon-Johnson real estate joint venture."

In fact, there was one female analyst in the early days. Canyon had a lateral partner who was running a small hedge fund on his own, and his sole employee was a woman my age, one of the sharpest, most original thinkers I have ever met. She was stuck outside of the main trading floor, literally sitting in a tiny cubicle in the hallway. Anyone who came to the office assumed she was the receptionist. Visitors would dutifully introduce themselves and ask for their meeting or a conference room. Deliverymen dropped boxes by her chair. Lunch caterers set the food on her desk. She hated it. She would pretend not to hear, and they invariably concluded that she was deaf, rude, or both, which, as I now reflect on it, cannot have been an optimal introduction to Canyon. In any case, the first time I spoke to her was, naturally, to ask where the bathroom was, under the same presumption.

"I am an option and risk arbitrage trader," she snapped, scornful.

"Sure, I know that," I lied, "but don't you go to the toilet?"

She eventually became the second female Canyon analyst (I was the first) and moved from the hallway to the open trading floor. We sat next to each other for years, until she quit around 2006. We are still best friends. I only recently asked her, while hiking on a beautiful Monday morning, marveling at *not* being in an office (the elation never stops, if you ask me), why she left Canyon after eight years as a successful and respected risk and convertible arbitrage investor. "Deep down," she said, "I wasn't convinced I was competent. Yes, there were the occasional sour trades, the office politics, the stress…but the killer was not finding support to believe in myself." Understand, she is one of the quickest minds I know. Yet she suffered from the impostor syndrome attributed prevalently to women by the inventor of the term, Dr. Pauline Clance.[2] She added, "Besides, there was no one to look up to as a female executive at the firm or anywhere on Wall Street and no road map. And the added ugly burden that, as a young woman, I felt the need to be physically attractive and feminine if I wanted a chance at finding a partner and having a family." It is somewhat a vicious circle: not enough women as role models, which leads, at least partly, to doubting one's own competence, which cannot be assuaged by female peers. And if there happens to be, oh miracle, one other woman, it is hard to be supportive rather than competitive if, looking around the office, there only seems to be room for *one of your kind.* It is not so much a glass ceiling as it is a quicksand floor.

As a woman at Canyon, but even more so as a foreigner, I felt slightly incongruous, not unlike my summer as a foreign exchange student in a Japanese family or my first job as a coincidental banker in New York. The feeling was familiar, perhaps even comfortable. Somehow, I feel comfortable being uncomfortable. I stood in an environment where I was an anomaly but not the object of sexism. Being an outsider can be freeing in many ways; being the object of prejudice never is.

FOREIGN "IDEARS"

I feel reasonably confident that moving to a different country was liberating. My Frenchitude gave me excuses and gave others leeway to accept my differences. Embarrassing or awkward behaviors and mystifying turns of speech found a natural explanation and went no further than the fact that, being French, I knew no better.

The rules seemed to apply less. The judgments came down less hard and less often. Or maybe I just was oblivious to it all. It was such a convenient cover-up. I kissed the air often in the first few years, when a vague acquaintance, sometimes even the odd business relation, approached to say hello, expecting a handshake instead of a double kiss. (Is it me or do Americans kiss a lot more these days? Did I single-handedly modify a code of behavior?) Among many other words, I cannot pronounce "idea"; it comes out "idear." You would be amazed at how many concepts, notions, thoughts, theories, and visions I've had over the years, but very few ideas. I surprised a few colleagues with the honest but mistaken assumption that "nerd" and "stud" were synonyms, the use of "pizza-faced" in lieu of "dumb," or the loose but evocative translation of classic French slang, which I have an encyclopedic knowledge of. Some of my favorite sayings include "calling a cat, a cat"; "pissing in a violin"; and—please excuse my French—"fucking a fly" (nitpicking). I revolted many with my diet choices, from rabbit to sweetbreads. But beyond these trivialities was the deep advantage that I could use my outsider status as a fallback for serious matters. Thus doing, the sky was the limit.

A colleague, years after I joined Canyon, called me the court jester. I cherished the title (another one called me a kamikaze, which is a lot less flattering, although in a similar vein). The jester's role is to amuse the king while speaking the truth. While the court is bowing to the royalty on high and going along with whatever it thinks the king wants to hear, the jester, under the cover of his (or her) weirdness, actually speaks freely and frankly, offering controversial or even offensive insights. He or she has a license to disagree.

As my time progressed at Canyon, I used that license more and more during the Monday morning meetings where the partners talked about various aspects of the business. I would often be the sole partner sticking my neck out, debating or opposing. Our discussions and arguments mostly revolved around portfolio construction, market positioning, and specific investments and trades. However, when politics came up—particularly when politics and economics became entangled, which occurred increasingly often over the last twenty years—I regularly found myself on the lonely side of the argument. The war in Iraq under George W. Bush, triggered by Iraq's supposed possession of weapons of mass destruction, presented a particularly trying period. France was a striking dissenter to the American effort to gather support for the war, which sparked a potent anti-French sentiment among administration officials (no doubt shared by many Americans). Bob Ney, the Republican in charge of building operations for the Capitol complex, gave the order to remove the word "French" from the menus of the cafeterias of the House of Representatives and encouraged restaurateurs around the country to do the same, in a symbolic and patriotic effort to spite their old ally. French fries would become "freedom fries," French toast "freedom toast." (There was more enthusiasm for renaming the fries.) A spokesperson for the French embassy, and mark this, a woman, observed reasonably and not without humor, that they were "working these days on very, very serious issues of war and peace, life or death. We are not working on potatoes."

No weapons of mass destruction were ever found in Iraq. Do you know what they did find shortly after this startling revelation? Enough evidence of lobbying corruption, document falsifications, and even conspiracy to send Bob Ney to prison for thirty months. I bet he wasn't served freedom anything in there, fried or toasted.

During the Iraq War and many other politically turbulent times, I felt like persona non grata in the office. It was depressing and isolating. Another such time was the 2009 European crisis that left Portugal, Italy, Ireland, Spain, and Greece in a crippled financial state, at odds with Germany, threatening the very existence of the European Union. It quickly rekindled questions about why "these" people hated each other so much that they had massacred each other in two wars. The silver lining of being a European pariah was that I knew the history of the European Union, which led to a helpful contrarian—and ultimately correct—view of the viability of Europe and its currency. The foundation of the E.U. is not economic, it is political. It was designed by two visionary politicians, intellectuals, and heroes of the French Resistance during the Second World War to permanently cement together the fate of France and Germany by merging their most important industrial sectors, coal and steel. They believed that would render war "not merely unthinkable, but materially impossible." This was but the first step in 1951 in the building of the European Economic Community (1957), the European Single Market (1993), and the creation of the Euro currency (2002). If there was one thing I was certain of, it was that the beacon of European peace would not be dismantled, even with the departure of one or more distressed members. The core would rally and stay together.

Several other topics were similarly divisive. Any discussion of taxes and healthcare made my blood boil. I swear, I am not the female Che Guevara of Wall Street. I do not believe everybody should be working for publicly owned capital. In fact, I vote center-right in France. However, I do believe in the government playing a pivotal role in society, particularly in wealth redistribution. I believe in paying taxes and using that money for public good (whether that happens more or less efficiently is of course up for debate). I believe that money is self-reinforcing, not self-propagating. I believe that we should redirect some amount of money to the poorest, the neediest, and the weakest. The idea that we are all equal and that the harder working or smarter people will naturally come out ahead is simply a childish one, most likely that of a Caucasian upper-middle-class male child.

The concept of social mobility that all Americans cherish and many still believe in has largely disappeared. Until the 1980s, there may have been room for people to move up, to get ahead, to become rich. Today, it is more an anecdotal than a statistical possibility. Over the last forty years, wealth has crystallized at the top of the pyramid and will just not move anymore. Yet somehow, 70 percent of Americans (according to a July 2019 Gallup poll) still view the American Dream as achievable. I have a bridge to sell them. Many studies point to the death of American upward mobility starting with the Reagan years. An excerpt from a 2016 paper by University of Massachusetts researchers concludes, "Across the distribution of educational attainment, the likelihood of moving to the top deciles of the earnings distribution for workers who start their career in the middle of the earnings distribution has declined by approximately 20% since the early 1980s." Harvard University economist Raj Chetty said in an interview, "People born in the 1940s or '50s were virtually guaranteed to achieve the American dream of earning more than their parents did. But that is not the case anymore. You see that for kids turning thirty today, who were born in the mid-1980s, only fifty percent of them go on to earn more than their parents did." Mr. Chetty is "arguably the best applied microeconomist of his generation" according to the American Economic Association, a researcher who has spent his career scientifically demonstrating that the American Dream is dead and finding ways to revive it. His Harvard venture, Opportunity Insights, includes

Bill Ackman as a financial backer. Other key players on Wall Street have taken notice. Ray Dalio of Bridgewater posted a LinkedIn article in April 2019 titled "Why and How Capitalism Needs to be Reformed," in which he points out that "Prime-age workers in the bottom 60% have had no real (i.e., inflation-adjusted) income growth since 1980. That was at a time when incomes for the top 10% have doubled and those of the top 1% have tripled."

Money is no longer circulating among social classes; it gets stuck at the top. Take large universities—Yale, Stanford, Harvard—all of which have multibillion-dollar endowments. As of this writing, Stanford's endowment is just over $25 billion, of which it invests a significant part in hedge funds. In fact, it was Yale University in the early 2000s that was instrumental in legitimizing and encouraging hedge fund allocations (as well as other types of alternative assets such as private equity) from institutional investors, through its endowment chief investment officer David Swensen. The Yale Model, also called the Endowment Model, marked a turning point in the growth of hedge funds and their ability to attract long-term capital.

What ensues, however, is a bizarre circle—whether virtuous or vicious is in the eye of the beholder. As a Stanford alumna, I had come to expect at the end of every year, along with Christmas, my bonus, and taxes, in that order, a knock on my door from the Stanford fundraising office asking me for money for their endowment. I usually agreed to donate, and they, through many intermediaries and tortuous paths, endeavored to invest their money, at least partly, in the hedge fund where I worked. Which dutifully proceeded to charge them large fees and in so doing, accumulated money for my next bonus. The next year, we did it all over again. This is but one example of how, at the highest echelons of the financial world, there exists a kind of *in vitro* wealth creation, a pass-the-ball money circle that mystifies me. Mind you, I still cashed my bonus check.

I don't want to leave the impression that I advertised blasphemous opinions in my first days at Canyon or marched into the partners' office blasting my devious views about the collateral damage caused by the capitalist system unless I was specifically asked. No, I am as opinionated and stubborn as they come, but even I knew to restrict my opinion to what I was hired to do: recommend investments and trades. But every one of these topics has important ramifications for building a portfolio and managing money. An armed conflict usually pushes investors toward the safety of treasury bonds and away from risky equities. Changes in taxes impact corporate profits and household income. Wealth distribution changes consumer spending, the most powerful motor of the American economy. How one interprets, understands, and forecasts these issues affects investment recommendations—and to fully grasp them, a plurality of opinions in the investment team is needed.

With experience, including a few market meltdowns, global crises, and promotions along the way, I found my voice; I was increasingly able to dissent, to push my points of view and assert my opinions. My court jester status cemented, building on a solid foundation of pigheadedness and irreverence that I mostly blame, and occasionally praise, my mother for.

MY MOTHER'S DREAMS

My mother was a survivor. She was born in Bucharest, Romania, to a well-off Jewish family. Her father was a prominent doctor and her mother a homemaker who oversaw a full staff of cooks, maids, and a revolving door of French or German or British governesses for my mother and her brother. Bucharest was known as the Paris of the East back then. When Nazism came to Romania during the Second World War, her father had to stop practicing medicine. The whole family wore the yellow star, but they avoided the concentration camps. Then, the Soviet Army moved in and by 1944, for all practical purposes, Romania fell under control of the USSR. As the Stalinist reign solidified into a terror regime in the Soviet Union, so did the government in Romania. My mother's house was seized and four or five families were forcibly crammed inside to share it. When Stalin died in 1953, a brief window opened for Romanian Jews to leave. My twenty-something mother had a distant uncle and aunt in Paris whom she begged for sponsorship, threatening that if they didn't help, she would commit suicide. She swore she meant it. They agreed. Escape she did, alone and destitute at first. Her father had died long before. She arranged for her mother to join her in Paris, and her brother emigrated to the U.S. The upper-bourgeoisie upbringing was long gone; she was a refugee, stateless and penniless. She picked up and started again. In the process, she somehow shaved a few years off her age on her French immigration papers, a trick that I now deeply wish to have pulled off when I moved to the U.S.

In Paris, she managed to study at the Beaux-Arts and became an architect. She could suffer fascism, communism, and poverty, but not a lack of education. She described Nicolae Ceaușescu, the despot of some twenty years who turned Romania into one of the most repressive totalitarian regimes in the Eastern Bloc at the time and whom she had met in her youth, as an "uneducated peasant"— that was the highest degree of her vitriol. She valued education not as a means to a successful career or an enviable salary, but as an end in itself. Thus, she was infatuated with the idea of her children studying on a university campus. Was the campus her romantic ideal of a holy place for intellectuals, a sort of ancient Agora where students, emulating Greek philosophers, peacefully paced together while discussing the greater ideas of life, the betterment of oneself and the improvement of the human race? I doubt she ever considered the amount of partying and boozing that goes on there, and I never burst her bubble, having partaken in none of it. Or so was my party line.

Her approach to religion was purely scholastic. She was Jewish, of course, but neither believed in the faith nor celebrated any Jewish holidays, rituals, or traditions. On the way to a Jewish friend's house to celebrate Passover, she once casually asked me if I had baked a cake for dessert. Sure, I said, and a pork roast for an entrée. Yet she had read, and made me read, every notable book about the Holocaust and Gulag, from Primo Levi to Arthur Koestler, from Aleksandr Solzhenitsyn to Yevgenia Ginzburg, and a special mention to Vasily Grossman. Did she love these works because they covered the markers of her life or because she felt it was an important part of the drama of human society? I never asked. She chose only biographies of survivors, individuals who went through the horror that she went through and much worse and came out on the other side. They made it. She cherished the strength of the human spirit, which she had in abundant quantity. She was a small woman, but of exceptional physical and mental endurance and unbreakable optimism. A true Latin, as Romanians are, she had spectacular mood swings, going from furious to jubilant, loving to hating. She was extremely assertive and quick to quarrel if she felt wronged. Heated arguments were business as usual in my house, and my brother and I grew up accustomed to, even comfortable with, conflicts and clashes. To this day, if challenged to a fight, I gleefully enter the ring in the spirit of a good debate.

I also inherited her endless curiosity, her epicurean desire to see, to go, to hear, to visit, to taste, to enjoy. I too emigrated for a better opportunity—although of my own volition and under indisputably more comfortable circumstances. My husband is an immigrant as well. The pattern may continue for generations. My elder son, when he was seven years old, gravely asked where he should go, what country he should move to as an adult. "You can go anywhere," I said. Great help, I was. He paused, judging quietly the inadequacy of my answer, and said, "I don't want to go to Iraq because there's a war there." I congratulated him on a judicious decision and agreed, "Cross Iraq off your list but anything else is fair game."

At this point, I should confess that I never dreamt of getting married and even less envisioned having children. As a little girl, I once had vague ambitions to become a great journalist, or a great pianist or a great firefighter—a great anything, as it were. The Parisian friends with whom I lost touch when I left France are invariably befuddled when they find out that I am married with two kids. I feel compelled to explain myself by adding that I worked on Wall Street at a killer hedge fund, so they concede, "At least you got one part of your life right."

Getting your life right requires luck and perseverance. I have both. Feeling lucky depends on how wide a lens you use to look at your life. I don't mean to say that I won the lottery, but if I consider the country and demographics into which I was born and the education and values I was given, my invariable conclusion is that I am a lucky girl indeed. But the choices to go to the U.S., stay, and stick with a heavily male-dominated business for two decades and aim for the top, those were mine.

Endurance and resilience are invaluable professional skills, as far as I can tell. They are not sexy; many asses claim them. But then again, when you feel tested, when you resolve to thrive in a place that feels strange, in an industry that doesn't include people who look, think, or act like you do, these qualities make a difference. They can transform being an outsider, behaving like an "other," or thinking as a contrarian into critical assets.

I am not only referring to investment cases, although I must point out here that I was, a decade later as the European debt crisis unfolded in 2009, the lone "native" voice in the office confidently and correctly affirming that neither Greece, nor Italy, nor Spain would leave the Eurozone or tank the currency. As a foreigner, I could also blissfully ignore and deeply distrust the conventions and stereotypes that often stifle American women. In her acceptance speech, Kamala Harris declared that her most important role is "Momala." Really? The former California attorney general, first Asian American female senator, first African American female presidential running mate is most proud of being a stepmother? Or could it be, rather, that she must conform to the politically correct stereotype that even successful women be primarily family focused, that even powerful women be foremost selfless caretakers?

I have no such qualms. Perseverance and the pursuit of self-interest? Yes, that goes for women too. I never apologized for, restrained, or disguised my professional ambition. The woman that Canyon Partners hired was not a good girl who chose to get along with people as her seminal virtue. I was a girl who was good at seeing what she wanted and convinced deep down that she could get it.

CHAPTER 4

STANDING UP

My wonderful paternal grandfather, a blue-collar factory worker from a cobblestoned village in the east of France, whom my mother routinely called a peasant when fighting with my father, once asked me what I did for a living. I work in finance, I said. "Do you sit, or do you stand?" he asked. I sat. He was impressed.

A hedge fund is not a bank, and I was not a teller, standing at a bank window to open checking accounts. A hedge fund is an investment firm entrusted with large sums of money pooled by a variety of investors, including high-net-worth individuals, private wealth advisory firms (also called family offices), insurance companies, endowments, pension funds, sovereign funds, banks, and many others. What sets a hedge fund apart is the way that it charges its clients (i.e., investors) for the service of managing their money, and the strategies it can employ to invest it.

Yes, everyone sits in a hedge fund; only the money stands out. The first person to exceed an annual income of $1 billion was a hedge fund manager—not an athlete, a movie star, or a CEO. Eddie Lampert earned $1.02 billion in 2004, almost fifteen years ago, according to *Institutional Investor*. If that was a shocking amount then, it is commonplace now. In 2019, the top fifteen hedge fund managers collectively made $12 billion; five of them made over $1 billion in earnings, according to Bloomberg. Here's how it works: A hedge fund charges investors two types of fees. The first is a management fee, usually 1 percent to 2 percent calculated as a percentage of the assets it gathers and invests. The second is a performance fee (also called incentive fee), usually 20 percent collected on the profit it produces, while the remaining 80 percent is returned to the investors. The point of this profit sharing is to align the interest of the hedge fund general partner (or owner, or manager), with that of its investors to produce the highest possible return. The effect of it, however, is to create towering revenues for the hedge fund manager. A fund that manages $1 billion makes $10 million per annum in management fees. By contrast, mutual funds only charge a small, single fee on their assets, usually around 0.30 percent, which would amount in this example to $3 million. In addition, if a hedge fund generates 10 percent return on assets one year ($100 million), it keeps 20 percent of the profit after the management fee ($100 million minus $10 million in management fee times 20 percent is $18 million) while the investors pocket the rest. A fund of this size would be considered small (consider that Canyon managed $25 billion in assets in 2019) and needs an investment staff of fewer than ten, who share the vast majority of this $28 million profit, or almost $3 million a head.

Over time, the fee structure of a hedge fund can perversely cease to be a profit incentive and become instead a driver of asset size. Say the same hedge fund has grown to $20 billion in assets but is having an extremely poor year and produces zero return. The management fee alone is $200 million a year while the performance fee is zero. The investment staff has grown to thirty people from ten, and while operating expenses have grown (marketing, investor relations, accounting, legal, compliance, IT), the investment group still keeps the vast majority of the profit—call it $5 million per investment analyst. Without producing a single penny in profit, the average earnings per analyst almost doubled. In other words, it is more lucrative to be a $20 billion fund that produces no return than a $1 billion fund that produces a 10 percent annual return. Scale has dwarfed skill. In fact, a fascinating 2009 study by Bing Liang and Christopher Schwarz ("Is Pay for Performance Effective? Evidence from the Hedge Fund Industry") confirmed, "Our results show that the primary objective of hedge fund managers is to hoard assets."

Call them hoard funds.

The second distinguishing factor of a hedge fund is its investment strategy, or mandate. Because hedge funds are private partnerships that are not subject to the same standard of Securities and Exchange Commission (SEC) regulation as mutual funds, they can invest however they see fit. The nomenclature originally came from a fund created by Alfred Winslow Jones around 1950, which comprised long positions in stocks he deemed undervalued and short positions in stocks he deemed overvalued. Born in Australia but raised in the U.S. and educated at Harvard, he first joined the Foreign Service Association and then worked for *Fortune Magazine*, reporting on stock "technicians." He is credited with being the father of the hedge fund industry by cleverly designing a fund to perform well regardless of—or, in finance terms, uncorrelated to—the general stock market direction by being "hedged" (as in hedging a bet, or betting on both sides of a coin flip). If Winslow was around today, he might go long Tesla stock and short General Motors, betting that the electric vehicle market and its corporate leader will take over the traditional oil-gobbling vehicles. As a result, he would expect to reap profits from Tesla's stock soaring and GM's tumbling. The name stuck despite becoming a misnomer when hedge funds started investing in a wide variety of assets and strategies beyond long and short stocks, and not necessarily uncorrelated to the market. Today, there are innumerable types of hedge funds: equity (long/short, long, activist); emerging markets; event-driven; macro; convertible arbitrage; merger arbitrage; fixed-income arbitrage; macro; distressed; and the list goes on. Canyon combines a number of these strategies, but with deep roots in high-yield bonds and distressed investing—that's what I did, sitting in my office, a glorified nomenclature for a sad little cubicle at first, turning a decade later into a plushy furnished suite with a view—rather than standing at a bank window, bless my grandfather.

Distressed investing and high-yield bonds used to be called, before we polished the terminology, vulture investing and junk bonds. I resented the ugly bird and garbage analogies as truly lacking any glamour. Besides, the point of distressed investing is not to feast on the decaying leftovers of other investors; we do, but that's only the start, not the end. Stressed and distressed (the only difference between the two qualifiers being the immediacy of bankruptcy) investing *begins* with buying the bonds or the loans of a company under severe operational or financial duress, either within bankruptcy or on the verge of filing for bankruptcy.

These bonds will remain worthless unless we manage to clean up the company through a capital restructuring or an operational turnaround or, more likely, both. The goal is to make the company viable and profitable again with a sustainable financing plan, thereby increasing the value of its securities. As such, if one is looking to biology for an analogy, a cleaner fish provides a service to other aquatic life such as sea turtles, manatees, or octopi (its "client" in biology parlance) by removing dead skin and ectoparasites, thus restoring health (and "value" in financial terms). Is it selflessness, cooperation, or exploitation? Whatever the motivation, this symbiosis is mutually beneficial. A cleaner fish thrives by making its client healthy. Yes, the best description for many distressed investors I have met over two decades is undoubtedly that of the cleaning goby or *Elacatinus*: large head, soft body, dorsal fins lacking spine, and of relatively small size. I don't ask intimate questions, but it's less than ten centimeters, according to Wikipedia.

THE OPEN SEAS OF INVESTING

Hedge funds make money by capitalizing on market inefficiencies, which are always fleeting opportunities. In the short term, once enough funds exploit them, the inefficiencies vanish and with them, the sources of alpha (alpha is the part of return that is uncorrelated to the market; beta is the part directly correlated to it). Over the long term, technology (allowing financial statements to be accessible online), regulations (requiring the same disclosure to all investors), and competition have eroded many inefficiencies, and hence profitable prospects, forever. Let me be specific.

Back in the '90s when I started, one of the most salient inefficiencies was informational. Information was scarce, slow, and expensive to obtain. It was only in 1996 that the SEC required all reporting companies to file their financial results electronically on a system called EDGAR. Until then, SEC reports were filed on paper and had to be requested as a physical copy. Although institutional investors had an internal library where documents were stored on diskettes and accessible in a matter of hours, others had to rely on their brokers or wait for the reports in the mail. It meant that some operators knew the financial numbers before others and could use the time lag as a strong competitive edge in making decisions and investing profitably.

It took nine years for the SEC to mandate that all reports (not only annual and quarterly financials but also amendments, supplements, and ownership reports) be filed and made accessible on EDGAR. Today, once filed, a document is immediately available to anyone with internet access. Not only can you access EDGAR from your phone, but most companies, public or private, have a website where they instantaneously post and make free of charge all their reports, press releases, earnings presentations, conference calls, and investor relations material.

In addition to being limited, information at the time was also selective. Regulation FD (fair disclosure) put an end to that inefficiency in 2001. The rule generally prohibits SEC reporting companies from disclosing nonpublic, material information to only a select group of investors. The information either must be distributed to the public at large, or, if it is released to a limited number of recipients, must include a confidentiality agreement that qualifies the recipients as insiders, and subjects them to trading restrictions. In plain English, if you are in possession of confidential information about a company, it becomes illegal to trade its stocks and bonds. Until then, management teams routinely gave heads-up information such as profit warnings, product development, or corporate strategy guidance during private conference calls and discriminating meetings. Large institutional investors condemned Reg FD as potentially harming disclosure (in reality, it would harm *their* ability to profit from selectively disclosed material information) and fought vigorously against the proposed rule. They argued that fair disclosure would lead to less disclosure. Nevertheless, in October 2000, the SEC promulgated Regulation FD.

As far as distressed investing went, bankruptcy proceedings and rulings are not required disclosure by the SEC and therefore the information was even harder to get, until the PACER system. PACER is an electronic public access service of U.S. federal court documents, which was set up on the web in 2001. It allows users to obtain case and docket information from, among other courts, the bankruptcy courts. This system was initially a pay-per-page system and so expensive (court documents are routinely Bible-thick) that it was prohibitive for most investors except hedge funds to acquire. Its fees have continuously decreased over the years, and multiple services, including corporate websites, now post court documents at no cost. Before then, few investors could access, and even fewer pored over, bankruptcy documents and data (such as the judge, attorneys, and trustees' information, claim registry, court scheduling, motions, hearings, and decisions). Instead, following and understanding the fate of a company in bankruptcy often required us hedge fund vultures to physically circle in the courtroom.

As I entered the hedge fund business in 1998, distressed investors still had an undeniable edge by getting all the information, getting it first, and getting it right. Even so, I was a cleaner fish lost at sea looking for an octopus client. I had no context in which to price a bond and no understanding of the arcane workings of a restructuring or bankruptcy case. I arrived in the office before the market opening, at 6:30 a.m. (a discipline that I kept until my very last day as a partner) and pored over financials, spreadsheets, and court documents. The trading floor was unlike any Hollywood scene of traders shouting orders. Rather, it resembled a library full of studious, brainy researchers. Now, I could be as studious as Bill Gates, but I just didn't know what I was looking for.

I came to love the investigating aspect of my job. For one thing, whereas a stock is not a particularly interesting security per se (the underlying corporation is interesting but not the instrument), junk bonds are fascinating creations. A stock is a stock, a slice of equity, a financial construct that doesn't change much apart from its dividend and the voting rights—a stock is, by nature, a voting share giving shareholders the crucial right to elect corporate directors and make their views known in different matters. But a corporate debt is a private contract with infinite variations. Even in a very well-established market like the U.S. leverage loan, junk bond, or investment-grade bond markets, there are meaningful divergences—sometimes very subtle, sometimes glaring—sufficient to separate a losing trade from a winning one. Corporate debt terms and conditions (maturity, coupon, covenants, ranking, collateral and a host of other factors) change all the time depending on the company, the industry, and market conditions.

Distressed trading is a game of strategy, positioning, power, and control. Corporations in bankruptcy or under financial stress often have a complex capital structure where equity holders, bondholders, loan holders, trade vendors, and a variety of parties have differing, often opposite economic interests. We ran computer simulations, scenarios, and projections and anticipated the moves of each player. Then, having evaluated the battleground, we would position ourselves strategically and select our weapon, the optimal security (or securities) to make a killing. It was like *Game of Thrones* minus the sex but with the profanity.

Investing is also executing a trade today with the calculated expectation that it will be worth more someday; in other words, it is predicting the future. I don't mean emulating Nostradamus; I mean envisioning the different paths that a business, stakeholders, an industry, a market, or a bankruptcy judge may follow, and weighting them with appropriate probabilities to deduce a likely future value. I would investigate the ideas and leads of our firm's head of research and our partners; analyze financial statements; cold-call management teams, competitors, vendors, other investors, and former employees to understand a company; visit plants and stores; poll clients; try products—anything to form a reliable picture of the battlefield. Restaurants, particularly food chains, later came under my coverage of industries. My mandatory French reverence for the culinary arts rendered due diligence of these companies particularly upsetting. Not to be graphic, but I once paid a heavy intestinal price for my thoroughness during a trip to evaluate HomeTown Buffet, as it was nearing bankruptcy. It served as a warning when I dealt with Joe's Crab Shack. Years later with Outback Steakhouse, then Applebee's, I smartened up: I sent my analyst as food taster. It would have been heresy then to voice what I am about to write now, but it is a load off my chest. I am not fully convinced that restaurant chains are of value to humanity. On the other hand, I have warm and fuzzy feelings toward household linens, which I also became familiar with under strained professional circumstances. I once flew to Kannapolis, North Carolina—proclaimed with more than a whiff of endearment as "the town that towels built"—to visit the largest textile plant of the then-failing (and now long-defunct) Pillowtex. Upon my return to the office, and civilization at large, one partner asked me to draw a diagram of the entire process, from the cotton ball to the pillowcase. And so it went. Every piece of information got me closer to an informed assessment, just as every bit of intelligence on the environment, the terrain, and the enemy shapes a military operation.

A widespread misconception about the hedge fund profession is that you must be either a math geek or a sleazy dealmaker to succeed. Generating new ideas, innovative thinking, having flashes of intuition that connect the dots—that is what helps a company refinance a bond in a tough market. Being a good listener and open-minded, capable of boiling down complicated facts into simple explanations, negotiating and multitasking—that is what brings investors to coalesce around a plan of reorganization and out of bankruptcy. What goes for distressed investing, which was my primary specialty, goes for investing in general. Over the years, I invested in risk arbitrage, equities, interest rates, municipal bonds—you name the asset class, other than currencies and commodities. My conviction is that the job of investing is highly creative and that the qualities it requires are imagination, ingenuity, and guts. All qualities that women have in equal quantity with men.

"COOPETITION"

During my first three years at Canyon, I was an executor rather than an investor, a position that I tolerated with the patience of a type A, top-of-her-class overachiever: poorly. At the time, there were five analysts and the head of research, all making recommendations to the two founding partners. I was the most junior and one of two women at the firm for a few years. Later, a few women came and went while I rose in seniority. My experience is hardly unique. A McKinsey study on the gender gap[3] reports that "women and men in financial services begin their careers at parity, making up roughly equal portions of entry-level staff, but higher up the ladder, women account for only 19 percent of positions in the C-suite." I was not necessarily smarter or more competent. But I did believe—still do—that I was as smart and competent as my average male peer, and probably more than quite a few. This conviction was key to a career aspiration and the resilience to chase it. At a minimum, you must believe in your own ability to perform a job in order to pursue it. The hurdle for many women is the cultural preconception that skills in mathematics, and related fields like finance, are associated with masculinity. This gender bias, in turn, leads women to arbitrarily underassess their abilities to perform at the highest seniority level in a finance career and consequently opt out of it; men overrate their competence level and jump right in.

At the time, I didn't have any discretion to trade, nor my own portfolio. I found it profoundly vexing although in retrospect, it was completely fair. No investors would ever want their money single-handedly invested by a freshman who'd been at it for so short a time. Investing is a craft, not a gift. It requires some talent, but mostly practice and experience. Although I have the patience of a mosquito, I could already see the arc bending toward one day being able to take ownership of my positions. The goal was not only to have an opinion on an idea that the partners had assigned to me, but to have an idea they had not thought of themselves. These came about through some combination of lateral thinking about another investment, discussions with companies, lawyers, investors or sell-side analysts, business articles, political events, industry conferences, you name it. I wanted it badly. My mind was constantly on alert for the next trade, the big one I would sell to the partners so they would bet on me. A splendid trade does you no good if the higher-ups don't put up the capital. This was not the Stanford Investment Club anymore. To get ahead, I had to produce, stand up for my ideas, and make money in positions with my name on them. It was highly competitive and became increasingly so as the firm grew in assets and in people.

Why competitive? For one thing, there is a defined amount of capital to be invested. If one analyst is gutsy and convincing enough to push for a $100 million investment, there's that much less money for everyone else to use. The more capital that is put behind your trade recommendation, the more profit you stand to make on a winning bet—or conversely, to lose on a zombie position (that is, one that leads to dead money). Everyone is jostling to deploy as much capital as they can.

Over time, perversely, competition mounts as the size of assets under management grows, particularly past the threshold of several billions. Sure, there is more capital for each idea, but at the same time, there's also only a finite number of industries, of companies, of distressed situations with enough scale and potential return to deploy those billions of dollars attractively. The investment universe becomes too small for that much money. Analysts start stepping on each other's feet and getting in each other's face. I had many such kerfuffles over the years; I remember a few. I would not say I enjoyed them, at least not all of them, but I never shied away either. I regarded them simply as good opportunities to plant a flag of determination and mark my territory in a male-dominated, competitive environment.

The first occurred over a telecom trade within the first two years of my employment. I covered the wireless industry when it was in its infancy, and I was convinced I had uncovered a gem in the high-yield bonds of American Tower, an intriguing new company that owned and operated a few thousand cell phone towers. As wireless service became popular in the late '90s and picked up subscribers, telecom operators added geographic coverage, which required building more towers to support their network and transmit the cell signals. Yes, young readers will be dismayed at the horror of it. There was a time when a large swath of the country had no wireless coverage at all. That little company, incidentally, is worth over $100 billion and operates one hundred eighty thousand cell sites today—back then, it was a growth venture. Expanding so fast, in fact, that it was teetering on the verge of default, having financed its rocketing growth with debt it could barely afford. Yet the business model was solid, scalable, and predictable; all it needed was time and perhaps some creative liability restructuring. The rub was this: the company had also issued convertible bonds, which, as the name indicates, are unique in that they allow the holder to convert them into stock at a predetermined time and price. A more senior analyst who covered the convertible market had made the pitch ahead of me and bought them. The high-yield bonds were clearly superior in my estimation; we needed to swap out of the convertible into the junk bonds. The partners agreed but the analyst dragged his feet to sell. I felt wronged. What started as a civil conversation on merit degenerated into a yelling contest.

I'm afraid I used insensitive words. It is conceivable that a smidge of hot temper and impatience found their way into my rant. Once we executed the swap, we never mentioned the outburst and got along smoothly, as indeed we had to, for the long-term sake of the company. For the record, I salute my ex-colleague for a well-coordinated trade.

Next, I had a brawl with a colleague who did not have my tenure but was older and presented himself as the airline expert. By then, airlines and aircraft had been my specialty for several years at Canyon, and I was a well-established investor in the sector. I suspected him, rightly or not, of going behind my back to make recommendations to the partners. He was advising to buy a United Airlines bond that I had already analyzed and rejected as poor value, having painstakingly appraised each of the twenty-five aircraft included in the collateral and concluded that they were hardly worth the mortgage against them. I didn't mind—indeed, I welcomed—a discussion about my work, as long as it was a full-frontal debate. I marched into his office with the mindset and physical agitation of a female lion protecting her cubs. "Don't ever, ever say anything to the partners about my positions without going to me first," I told him, loud enough for the entire trading floor to hear. I certainly used immodest vocabulary and unfocused words. I didn't let go after what I deemed a lame denial and improbable explanation; that was *my* air space. My animal instinct called for protecting the turf and standing up. The bond was never brought up again, by the partners or by my colleague. Which is why, looking back many years later, the story became slightly puzzling. On reflection, I wonder if the guy was really a sneaky upstart or if I made up the treacherous move in a small fit of paranoia. The latter is entirely possible. Regardless, I am awfully glad I leveled with him.

Years later, the shipping sector, which I also covered, went through a bust and provided a plethora of distressed opportunities.

However, our London office argued that because these companies were generally headquartered in Greece, Cyprus, or some non-U.S. tax haven, or had bonds traded in London, they had first dibs. You must be kidding, I said. What about companies that exported products or services outside of the U.S.? Were they off-limits too? Or companies with an international subsidiary or office? How about a foreign CEO? It was war, my positions, my portfolio, my territory. I was Napoleon, Canyon was Trafalgar, and history would be rewritten. I would win the naval battle.

One of the partners called it "coopetition," a portmanteau of cooperation and competition. That's fine when you are a man standing at the top. I felt I needed to kill (and do it early) the antiquated notion of some male colleagues that although women are hardworking and make good analysts, when the time comes to be an influencer, to champion their ideas and back their own advancement, they will fold. If anyone thought that I was vulnerable and would stand by silently—let alone cooperate—while someone stole my thunder, they were mistaken.

An analyst nicknamed me "the Velvet Hammer." My younger son at age ten described his mother as "nice, with a tendency to go nuclear." I deeply believe that I had to be more forceful, more aggressive, more persistent, more willing to put everything on the line than my male peers did. Did I ever worry that I could appear obnoxious instead of strong, unpleasant instead of competitive? Not really. Naturally, I am well aware of the absurd decorum requiring that women who want power should also be nice and that they should temper ambition with warmth, as recommended by a Harvard Business Review study[4] (which allegedly is not targeted at women but the message can hardly be missed), and that success generally translates into unlikeable when associated with the feminine gender. But here is the genuine beauty and justice of the investment job for outsiders: the point is to make money, consistently and over the long term. In the end, the market, not people's perceptions of who you are, is the supreme judge, with no further appeal. I was called a few savory epithets over the years, including ballbuster, bad cop, and my personal favorite, Saint Pit Bull. I find them rather humorous and the last one particularly endearing. I saw some men in the business skate by on their relationships, their small talk, and insinuate themselves as birds of a feather with investors, management teams, and other analysts because they *are*. They sit in a room full of people who look, act, and think like them. I could not. It took me a lot more effort, rehearsal, and preparation to attract capital for my ideas, convince a restructuring committee, or win over an investor. This is naturally a subjective perspective, and perhaps the rebuttal is that my ideas were simply not as good. It is possible, but not systematically likely. My hunch was confirmed when, recently, I came upon a research study[5] by a finance professor from Northeastern University who studied data from 1994 to 2013 and concluded: "Surviving funds with at least one female manager have better performance than male-managed surviving funds, consistent with the idea that female managers need to perform better for their funds to survive. Yet, female-managed surviving funds have fewer assets under management than surviving male-managed funds." Then comes the nail in the coffin: "Our results suggest that there are no inherent differences in skill between female and male managers, but that only the best performing female managers manage to survive." In other words, in order to survive, a female-run hedge fund must outperform its male competitors while doing so with fewer assets.

I must be honest, though. For much of my early years at Canyon, I hardly gave a thought to the gender conundrum or the issues that *other* women faced. Being a foreigner, I was quite used to feeling out of place and uncomfortable, particularly in the early years. The impostor syndrome, which I did experience, was naturally kept in check by my oversized ego. I did believe, in the final analysis, that I was worthy of the job. And so I single-mindedly and somewhat blindly focused on making money for the firm.

CHAPTER 5

SWIMMING IN OPPORTUNITIES

I would not recommend throwing a novice hedge fund analyst into a devastating financial crisis, the sort that ruins industries, disrupts capital markets' order, bankrupts countries, and threatens decades-old political systems. I merely encourage it. It builds character, polishes a contrarian mind, and sheds a completely new light on the meaning of downside. Ask any junior analyst to quantify the risk of a trade—any trade—that he is pitching, and regardless of the asset class, industry, market direction, hedging strategy, or economic stage, the answer you will get is, in my experience, 10 percent.

Always. The human mind cannot conceive, and the human body cannot stomach, the pain of losing more than that. If you live through one or more economic earthquakes, however, you learn that it is a miracle to lose only that. On the other hand, provided you do survive these shocks, they offer unrivaled opportunities to make money for the steady-minded.

I lived through three major crises. Granted, I was more or less sleepwalking through the 1998 Asian Flu crisis, feeling no particular uneasiness at the loss of half our value and assets, immune to the downright gloom in the office, and overall having a rather jolly time observing the carnage. It was almost as if my mother were right when she said at the time, revealing her near incomprehension of my job and my inability to explain it to her, "Don't you worry, Dominique, it's not *your* money." By the 2001 telecom crisis, let alone the 2008 Great Recession, it very much was.

The turn of the century first saw the burst of the dot-com bubble, in itself a relatively contained crash, mostly hitting the Nasdaq. Truthfully, I was not unhappy to witness the demise of a market that I had hardly understood and never invested in but had suddenly transformed everyone into a trading expert. My most humbling experiences were to listen to my hairdresser, dental hygienist, or OB-GYN describe how much money they made in stock picking. When the question invariably came, "What do you do?" I was always in a position of weakness. First off, either my hair was dripping, my mouth was wide open, or my legs were spread apart. Second, I had to confess that, although it in fact was my profession to invest, I had never bought a dot-com stock in my life. I had no hot tip to share. No insight into the value of an eyeball—back then, one measure of future profitability was simply the number of visitors to a website (there weren't subscribers or even customers at first). Attempting to explain that my specialty was distressed investing seemed rather pathetic and unnecessarily defensive.

The telecom crisis, which promptly followed the dot-com fall, was an entirely different beast. The media largely describes the dot-com and the telecom busts as one and the same. They were not. The latter was a financial calamity of epic scale with enormous consequences to all market participants, shaking not only the equity market (where the dot-com was mostly concentrated and the public mostly affected), but also the investment-grade bond, junk bond, and leveraged loan markets in the U.S. and beyond. This time around, it affected me. By then, I was no longer the new girl.

I had investments and positions of my own. When some of them came crashing down, every inch of my body ached, and I longed for the empathy that I had been curiously incapable of showing a few years earlier. Still, the proliferation of bankrupt companies in a wide variety of sectors proved to be an invaluable training ground, giving me the opportunity to rise up and become my own investor, develop my own style, and eventually my own expertise.

THE TELECOM IMPLOSION

In early 2001, the first signs of the telecom cracks appeared, right on the heels of the dot-com crash, which took the Nasdaq from a peak of around five thousand in March 2000 down to two thousand in early 2001.

The story is a familiar one—nothing is ever new on Wall Street. Multitudes of start-ups sprang up following the 1996 deregulation of the telecom industry. They undertook massive capital expenditures to develop and upgrade data and wireless networks using some version of the mantra "build it and they will come." Too few customers came, they came too late, and the proverbial hockey stick-projected growth in cash flow (let alone profit) failed to materialize. Companies began to fall on hard times when investors who had wholeheartedly financed the expansion until then suffered losses in the dot-com crisis, and became reluctant to extend further capital. Thus started the demise of the cash-hungry telecom companies, leveraged to the hilt and dependent on investors' appetite for their equity and debt to continue funding their business model.

Michael Powell, who later became chairman of the Federal Communications Commission, put it succinctly:

Companies in all sectors of the telecommunications industry, from wireline to undersea to wireless, across the globe and with global ambitions, set out to build national and global networks—some, as we all undoubtedly recall, by digging up streets to lay fiber, some through acquisition, some by bidding billions of dollars for spectrum, some by investing in foreign markets—to win the race to stay ahead of expected demand. In so doing, telecommunications companies throughout the world amassed a staggering amount of debt in building near identical networks. As we have painfully come to find out, the ambitious demand projections for network capacity did not materialize.

Telecom equipment makers provided vendor financing that they couldn't recoup and they went south. Long-distance and local telephone carriers got into deep trouble due to competitive offerings. At least a dozen companies filed for bankruptcy in 2000, and the trend soon extended to larger companies throughout the industry. Long-haul fiber-optic, cable-TV, satellite, internet, and wireless providers, you name it, were facing oversupply and disappointingly slow demand; they were all affected, and many were destroyed. It is impossible to overstate the depth of the abyss. From around September 2000 to 2002, the Dow Jones telecom index dropped 86 percent and the wireless index 89 percent. A telecom calamity.

In 2002 alone, WorldCom, Global Crossing, Qwest Communications, XO Communications, and Adelphia all went bankrupt. Companies that were once darlings of the markets—like Covad, Focal Communications, McLeod, Northpoint, and Winstar in the local phone business; 360 Networks in fiber optic, cable, and internet; and nTelos, NextWave, and Pinnacle Holdings in wireless—were no more. Younger readers will not even recognize their names. The telecom crash gave rise not only to an unprecedented number of bankruptcies, but also bankruptcies of unprecedented scale. Of the biggest twenty bankruptcies, half of them occurred during the telecom and telecom-related crisis.

I was involved in many of these cases. It was a bankruptcy investing boot camp. Every morning would bring a fresh crop of dire situations in what would form, over a period of two years, an extensive course in corporate restructuring.

Equity investors lost $2 trillion of value by the end of the year in the telecom industry alone out of a total $7 trillion market capitalization. But for Canyon and hedge funds involved in distressed, the golden goose had landed.

FIELD DAY OR BLOODBATH?

In 2002, over $400 billion was listed in public companies' prepetition liabilities (their obligations before they file for bankruptcy). This figure was up a full 50 percent from 2001, and up *400 percent* from 2000. If you combine 2001 and 2002, 600 public companies with $667 billion in assets went bankrupt. It was unprecedented. As a relative sense of measure, the average annual bankruptcy asset pool from 2003 to 2007 went back down almost ninefold to $75 billion.

At the time, hedge funds were relatively small (the number of hedge funds grew from three thousand when I started to approximately twenty thousand today), and distressed funds as an asset class, were even smaller. Total hedge fund assets in 2001 were only $371 billion ($455 billion in 2002) while, by most accounts, merely $15 billion of those assets was dedicated to distressed hedge fund strategies. To put it another way, in 2002 there were sixteen times more assets in bankruptcy than investors able to rummage through them. There was a flood of bankruptcies, and Canyon was swimming in opportunities. And it was not only telecom; unrelated industries were in equal disarray for different reasons. Around 2000, the movie exhibitors, having expended large amounts of capital to transform their multiplexes into megaplex theaters, were also experiencing enormous financial stress. Carmike Cinemas, General Cinemas, and United Artists filed for bankruptcy; Loews, AMC Theaters, and Regal Entertainment were posting losses and approaching creditors for potential relief and restructurings. The textile industry, affected by the competition from low-cost Asian producers, had its share of financial distress with Pillowtex, Burlington, and WestPoint Stevens, among many others, on the brink of, or filing for, bankruptcy as well.

It was then that my education in restructuring, reorganization, and the intricacies of bankruptcy started in earnest. I invested in dozens of companies that teetered on the brink of financial disaster before falling into bankruptcy. It was the biggest corporate mess since 1929, and I was the luckiest girl on Wall Street.

The world was littered with cheap assets and bargain companies—yet there were precious few investors with a deep enough understanding of the bankruptcy process to profit from buying companies that had fallen on hard times, along with the wherewithal, the mandate, and the money to take on the risk. It is no surprise then that, under these circumstances, the hedge fund industry vastly outperformed the market. For 2000, 2001, and 2002, the Standard & Poor's index returned negative 9 percent, negative 12 percent, and negative 22 percent while hedge funds returned positive 5 percent, positive 4 percent, and positive 3 percent. The subsection of hedge funds investing in distressed companies did even better: positive 2 percent, positive 20 percent, and positive 1 percent. If you had invested $100 in the S&P in 1999, you were left with little more than $62 by the end of 2002, while the same $100 invested in a distressed hedge fund grew to $123.

This remarkable outperformance whetted the appetite of investors and propelled an extraordinary multiyear expansion in distressed hedge funds. Assets almost doubled in each year of 2001, 2002, and 2003. It was this unique confluence of events that gave rise to an immensely profitable business—a tiny pot of money going after a giant pool of opportunities. The small size of the hedge fund industry versus the investment set was the decisive factor in their outperformance in these years. Today, some investors remain convinced that the outperformance can continue absent these conditions, but mark this, as it will be a recurring theme of this book: I beg to differ. From 2000 to 2008, distressed hedge funds beat the S&P and the high-yield indices in eight out of nine years. From 2008 to 2019, distressed funds did not beat the S&P in a single year and beat the high-yield index only in 2013 and 2014. If investors wish to continue paying the same fees in the face of illusionary market outperformance, let them.

I don't want to appear callous. I believed then, as I believe now, that distressed investing is a valuable service to the capital markets and the corporate world. The question of how much an investor should pay for the service is secondary. During these years, there was an abundance of wounded holders and forced sellers who needed or wanted to sell, at any price. For a market to work, there needs to be a buyer. It might be a buyer of last resort, at a terrible price, with vulture-like conditions, but a buyer nevertheless. That's what we were. We were no white knights rescuing damsels in distress. However, we showed up when everybody else was too scared to invest and roll up their sleeves. This was our battle plan: take control, restructure a balance sheet, equitize debt, cut pensions, trim vendors, cancel leases or shutter plants, all in the name of bankruptcy emergence and for the long-term health and profit of a company. It required the right research and analysis, creative and imaginative thinking about how to transform a business, and countless hours reading court pleadings and heavy investments in legal and financial advisors. If we ended up making a fortune, it was fair game given the outsized risk and expansive labor we took on.

A prevailing narrative is that distressed investors are like lions zooming in on prey, perceptive and ruthless predators going in for the kill, led by their natural instincts and a clear vision amid utter chaos. Or they are described as superhuman creatures—superheroes or super villains, depending on the oodles of money they win or lose. One media image that stuck is that of legendary distressed investor David Tepper, who kept a giant pair of brass testicles on his desk (and was said to rub them for good luck).

The truth is more nuanced. Here is an actual quote from David Tepper: "For better or worse we're a herd leader. We're at the front of the pack, we are one of the first movers. First movers are interesting, you get to the good grass first. Or sometimes the lion eats you." Everyone is scared and confused when the market tanks. No one sees opportunities on a consistent basis. The best investors make genius trades and disastrous bets. My point is that a hedge fund investor is just a regular guy (rarely a gal, unfortunately) who's trying to make money for investors and agonizes over investments, revisiting them every day, every minute until the market closes—in his shower, at dinner, and over the weekend—and repeats it all on Monday. The job is to look for value, bargains, and inefficiencies, which usually crop up when things are messy and ugly. There are times when you recognize early and unequivocally that the market is handing you a bargain; the telecom crisis provided such a backdrop. The reason why distressed funds made so much money back then is not because we were geniuses, not because of nerves of steel, wills of iron, or testicles of brass. It was because of timing, of the confluence of the newness and modest size of the business relative to the market structure and outlandish number of bankruptcies. In other words, happy circumstances.

THE WORLDCOM TOOTHACHE

My congenial dentist of twenty years is retiring this year, and of course he is nostalgic because I have excellent dental hygiene. He often jokes that if I keep it up, people will mistake me for an American. It got me thinking that if I had to put a face to the telecom crisis, it would be his, Dr. Medberry's. He once asked me if investing in distressed companies could be uncomfortable. The fellow digs into people's mouths and pokes around cavities. A set of rotten teeth gets him so excited that he can't wait to start the drill, for crying out loud. And he is asking *me* if I mind my job? First off, our jobs were quite similar, really. What deplorable decision-making led to the decay? Could it be reversed, fixed, or saved? Second, he was working on my teeth when WorldCom hit me. Because, let's be frank, it really did. A bad trade always feels viciously personal, as if it only happened to you. WorldCom hurt like a root canal.

In early 2002, at the height of the telecom crisis, I bought WorldCom bonds that were due to mature at the end of the year. The company was in disarray already. The stock had dropped from $60 per share in mid-1999 to around $10. In March, the SEC had opened an investigation into the company's accounting procedures and, specifically, some loans that WorldCom had extended to its officers. The CEO, Bernie Ebbers, had improperly borrowed $400 million from the company for his personal use. The board fired him. Nevertheless, the company had enough (by my calculations) liquidity on hand for the rest of the year. It produced sufficient cash flow to pay off my bonds and was highly motivated to keep the doors open to recoup its massive network investments. How bad could things go within a few months? I had paid only ninety cents on the dollar for the bonds, a bargain—so I thought—generously offered by sellers wary of a shady CEO character and an intrusive SEC inquiry. This type of investing has a name: picking up pennies in front of a steamroller. You'd better be sure of your payoff probability.

One afternoon in July 2002, after the market closed, I walked to my dentist's office on the same floor of our Beverly Hills office. My teeth cleaned and checked, I returned with a smile. Our head of research, an eminently phlegmatic and experienced high-yield investor, lifted his head from his screens and gently suggested that I go see the partners about WorldCom. Had the company paid my bonds early? I asked with an optimistic and very white grin. Not exactly, he said; they announced a $3.2 billion accounting fraud.

Just like that.

These were the days of widespread corporate malfeasance. When business prospects turned dire and bankruptcies piled up, some companies resorted to accounting tricks to buy time and fool investors, disguising expenses as capital expenditures (as did WorldCom), or booking capacity swaps between companies as true revenue (as did Global Crossing). Enron went bankrupt in 2001, the largest corporate bankruptcy ever at the time, followed by Conseco and Tyco Electronics; all were due to accounting fraud. This wave of swindling and deception crushed confidence in corporate America and gave rise, in 2002, to the Sarbanes-Oxley Act (cutely referred to as SOX), a federal law that established sweeping auditing and financial regulations for public companies.

The Enron bankruptcy was already a big deal, filing with $93 billion worth of assets. When my own golden goose kicked the bucket, it became the largest bankruptcy in U.S. history. WorldCom dwarfed Enron, with $144 billion in assets. It had eighty-eight thousand employees and owned sixty thousand miles of telephone lines worldwide.

People say you see your entire life replay in front of your eyes after a near-fatal accident. I'm pretty sure I saw Mademoiselle Bibi, my very first doll, sitting very pretty in the partners' office.

My bonds had dropped to twenty cents. WorldCom had simultaneously run out of cash and been caught cheating. Given the magnitude of the fraud, bankruptcy was the only option. I certainly didn't suspect the presence of these accounting shenanigans. I don't think I could have known, with all the research in the world, that they had booked certain expenses as investments to boost profit, although in retrospect, their abnormal profitability relative to their peers, including AT&T, could have raised doubts. However, there we were, trying to reassess the investment entirely. The job was to make a reasoned, cold-blooded decision. Could the rotten teeth be removed and the mouth saved and become functional again? The bad-apple CEO was gone. The accounting scam was out. What was the true profitability of whatever was left, and was there any upside?

The chances were good that the company would exit bankruptcy and return to profitability, albeit a greatly reduced one with less growth but also less debt. There were real businesses underneath the fraudulent coverup. Through its previous acquisition of MFS Communications, WorldCom was still a major internet service provider and its subsidiary MCI Communications made it one of the largest providers of business and consumer telephone service. The partners were familiar with MCI from their days at Drexel Burnham Lambert, when MCI had been a pioneer junk bond issuer. We doubled down. We bought significantly more bonds at twenty cents. The bankruptcy was long and complicated, starting with a new CEO from Compaq and the write-off of $80 billion of goodwill, intangible assets, property, and equipment. The next step was to settle charges of accounting fraud with the different parties: the SEC and the Oklahoma attorney general (where the campus was based). The plan was to emerge with a long-distance business under the MCI name and let the tainted WorldCom brand die in the process. In 2003, the bankruptcy judge approved MCI's plan of reorganization and the company emerged. MCI bondholders were paid about eighty cents on the dollar; WorldCom bondholders, about thirty-six cents. Almost two years after I had expected my payday, after considerably more aches and valuable lessons, we finally exited the WorldCom situation with a tidy profit. Not because of my original trade—very much despite it, in fact—but because, encouraged by my partners, I mustered up the gumption to accumulate a large amount of MCI bonds at the bottom. Bernie Ebbers was sentenced to twenty-five years in prison. He died shortly after his early release in December 2019.

Several years ago, my younger son inquired if I had ever lost a lot of money at work.

"Many times," I said dogmatically, "but what matters is to make more than you lose."

"When was the first time?" he insisted.

Why it is that he cannot ask how my winning trades paid for his Nintendo 3DS, I don't know. Anyway, wishing to impart some moral wisdom to my teenage scamp, I explained it all.

He just shook his head in consternation. "You should have seen it coming with a name like World Con," he said dryly.

CHAPTER 6

THE EETC ENCOUNTER

Everyone has a 9/11 story, particularly everyone related to Wall Street, the epicenter of the tragedy. Its geographic target was narrow, but with a wide-ranging impact on the financial world, both personal and professional lives. On September 11, 2001, I attended an investor conference in San Francisco. I was scheduled to fly to New York in the evening for a meeting the next day at Cantor Fitzgerald, One World Trade Center, 101st floor. My morning cab driver, when I mentioned the trip to New York, commented with some confusion that the airports, according to the radio, had just closed nationwide. When I walked into the conference hall, the crowd was overflowing outside the main meeting room, turned to the large TV screen, and it was not on the customary Bloomberg channel.

I stared at the shocking scenes on TV playing in a continuous loop, and it took watching the same set of images several times to grasp them. My female Canyon colleague was attending the conference, and it was an enormous relief to see a familiar face. We hugged and comforted each other. Being away on a business trip compounded the feelings of anguish and fear, and we ached to go home as quickly as possible. My husband, ever the planner, had the presence of mind to call Hertz in San Francisco immediately upon hearing the news. By the time we made it to the rental agency, we cut a line over a hundred people long desperately seeking a vehicle to take them home as well. We drove the six-plus-hour journey down the coast in sadness and confusion, alternating between trying to get information from the radio and to absorb what had happened to our world.

The next day, the partners, who had hitchhiked a ride back from New York on the private plane of a hedge fund chum, convened everyone in the conference room. "All right," one partner started, "I want you guys to call everyone you know in New York to see how they're positioned. We need to know what the smart people are doing, how they're going to manage the crisis and the moves in the market. I want to know what inefficiencies might come out of this."

I pondered privately and dubiously, I'm going to call people in New York *right now?* First of all, where am I going to call them? At home? Manhattan was under siege. If by some miracle I did get in touch with people I knew in New York, was I seriously going to ask how they were positioning their portfolio?

In retrospect, the partner was probably in as much shock as the rest of us. He was trying to hang on to some level of normalcy, of business as usual. It was reassuring to think there was a business to lead, a market to monitor, a portfolio to trade. I don't believe anybody called anybody—I certainly didn't. This partner was trying to replace personal and communal grief with business acumen and experience; hedge fund management, especially in distressed investing, is about being strategic and unemotional. While an extreme example, our business revolved around, literally, reconstructing from the rubble. And indeed, the aftershocks of 9/11 in the capital markets would provide Canyon with many trade opportunities in the years to come—and offer me my first big breakthrough.

BECOMING THE MAN

The stock markets remained closed for several days. On September 17, the New York Stock Exchange reopened and fell a whopping 7 percent. By the end of the week, the Dow Jones was down 14 percent. There was hardly any trading in corporate bonds. Entire sectors experienced deep sell-offs, particularly insurance and airlines. The government had closed the airports, and when they reopened, passenger traffic dropped 30 percent. Companies canceled or severely reduced business travel, the most profitable segment of the industry. The gravity of the situation clearly showed in American Airlines and United Airlines stocks, which fell 39 percent and 42 percent respectively on September 17. Within five years of the September 11 attack, almost all U.S. airlines (except Southwest and American Airlines) had filed for Chapter 11 (corporate reorganization) or Chapter 7 (corporate liquidation) bankruptcy, including US Airways (2002); United Airlines (2002); Hawaiian, Midway, and Evergreen (2003); and Delta Air Lines and Northwest Airlines (2005).

The seismic shock to the airline industry made it a logical investment area to follow for a distressed investor. Granted, it had always been prone to financial distress and bankruptcies and was naturally on the radar. From the '70s to the early 2000s, Continental had filed for bankruptcy twice and TWA three times—all told, from the Airline Deregulation Act in 1978 (which ended U.S. federal government control over fares, routes, and market entry of new airlines) until 2001, I counted 146 airlines going belly-up. As an industry, airlines suffer from being highly capital intensive (the expensive planes), subject to a frighteningly volatile main cost (oil prices), and an economically sensitive demand (passenger growth is correlated to gross domestic product growth). With the introduction of a free market, freshly formed airlines blossomed; passenger traffic increased but so did competition, pressure on fares, and, as a result, financial fragility. Many investors were familiar with these cases and possessed industry knowledge and experience; they had seen the movie before. But the airline crisis that followed the terrorist attack was global and endemic. No one had ever seen a movie like 9/11.

I was blissfully unaware of even the historical context. Until the partners asked me to investigate the capital structures of the U.S. airlines, I understood the industry as buying a ticket and getting on the plane, preferably in business class with a window seat that reclines into a full flat bed. I had no clue how planes were financed and no inkling that airlines commonly went bankrupt. There was a single airline in France when I grew up, and it was state-owned.

The partners' vote of confidence in assigning me this critical sector preceded many others in my twenty years at the company. I am enduringly grateful for it. It isn't that I was proactively mentored; no one was particularly invested in my personal success per se. They were doggedly committed, because it was the job, to making money. Each of us needed to tackle certain areas, and we were a small staff. The head of research was overseeing the entire portfolio, and my female friend and two other analysts specialized in the area of arbitrage (merger and convertible arbitrage) rather than corporate investments; that left me and one other distressed specialist. The choice was him or me—that was that.

I should add that assigning a specific industry to a particular analyst had not been part of the company's original organizational structure (and is not necessarily in the DNA of all hedge funds). The process by which we became specialized by industry came about around 2001 and solidified in the ensuing years; we had been industry agnostics until then. That year marked Canyon's foray into a new business with the issuance of a collateralized debt obligation, or CDO, a securitization product that I will come back to in a few chapters. Suffice it to say for now that it requires assembling a large portfolio of bonds, diversified by industry and companies. Hence, the head of research ascribed a handful of industries to each analyst with the mandate to find the best bonds for the CDO. The portfolio initially contained a heavy mix of telecom exposure. As the sector imploded in 2002, our portfolio quickly entered a crunch mode and required nimble and active trading to stay solvent. Our head of research did the brunt of the portfolio management, but he relied on the rest of us—rather than the partners, who, while they had the final say on trades, did not originate them—to swap out of the telecom sector into more creditworthy industries. The crisis fast-tracked us through the learning curve. I scrambled to become an expert in my initial industries (retail, consumer products, and wireless telecom) and acquired more trading expertise and independence along the way. When 9/11 hit, airlines—and later on, transportation—joined my coverage list.

In the area of airlines and aircraft, I became the man within a few years of 9/11—except as a woman, which was a notable rarity. Airline investor conferences were generally testosterone-overloaded—but less so than aircraft leasing, where more than the occasional conversation revolved around comparing the size of personal planes. Call me coy, but it was hard to mingle. It happened occasionally. At an annual Boeing meeting in Seattle, we were invited to try the flight simulators for two planes, the ancient and noble wide-body MD-80, and the new narrow-body 737. It would be terribly boastful to describe how I landed both birds perfectly while many of my male counterparts (including the brilliant and encyclopedic JP Morgan airline analyst) crashed, so I won't mention it.

The shipping sector, in which I started to invest almost fifteen years later, had a similar population, although this one was of the Viking variety, everyone standing six feet three inches tall and named Sven, Jan, or Thor. I joined such a group of all-male investors on a trip to Asia to visit shipbuilders. I had to call it quits midway. There was so much eating and drinking followed by overnight flights that my stomach threw in the towel after Japan and China. They continued to India. In Shanghai, a young Chinese engineer walked us through container ships and tankers the size of several large cathedrals, which filled me with both awe and terror of human ingenuity.

"Here," he said in English, indicating a warehouse, "is where we do the metal cutting. After that, over there, is the metal bending and welding areas." The others lingered and marveled while I walked with him two hundred meters, where shapes were already taking form, rising ten stories high to the sky. He turned to me proudly. "Here is where we do all our erections," he said.

"Congratulations," I said.

THE *TITANIC* IS NOT A PLANE

The airline bonds I stumbled upon in 2001 may not sound sexy, but then again, I bet neither did radioactivity in 1896. The encounter with enhanced equipment trust certificates (EETCs) was an epiphany, a personal Holy Grail, my Marie Curie moment. I am exaggerating a smidge, but to see and feel that *there is something there,* after considerable, often fruitless research and digging around was pure and unadulterated joy, even before sizing up any potential profit.

I don't believe Canyon had ever looked at EETCs. They were a new type of financing for airplanes that took off in the late '90s. They originate from an old structure used for railway boxcars and rolling stock, where the latter served as security for a loan, similar to a mortgage loan, in which the house is the collateral.

Aircraft financiers ingeniously figured they could use this basic structure while enhancing it, making it bankruptcy-remote, issuing senior and junior tranches of debt and equity, and adding a liquidity facility to allow interest payments even if the airline became bankrupt. The point of the enhancements was to make EETC bonds safer than regular airline corporate bonds, and to get them rated higher by the rating agencies, Moody's and Standard & Poor's. In turn, a higher safety rating would attract larger pools of money from traditional lenders like insurance companies and pension funds and allow for bigger and more frequent deals. It also presented tax advantages for investors in the equity of the structure. Northwest Airlines was the first to issue an EETC, in 1994. By 1997, at least eight transactions had been executed by major U.S. airlines, involving over ninety aircraft and $3.3 billion in bonds. Volume grew as aircraft securitization gained widespread acceptance, to a peak issuance of $15 billion as we entered 2001, and would have shown no sign of abatement absent the disaster of 9/11. However, with size, scale, and innovation also came complexity, a staple of securitization bonds.

Understanding the nuances of a particular securitization takes hundreds of working hours. Securitization bond indentures are notoriously thick, often exceeding thousands of pages. In the case of aircraft securitization, one feature is utterly unique and does not even relate to the bond itself, but to a specific section of the U.S. Bankruptcy Code, section 1110. EETC bonds are issued by a trust, which uses the money to buy the planes, rents them to the airline, and uses the rent money to pay bond interest. Section 1110 of bankruptcy code specifies that, if the airline files for bankruptcy, it faces a choice within a sixty-day period: either continue to make rental payments (with the bankruptcy court approval) if they want to use the aircraft, or default on the rent, which then enables the trust to repossess and dispose of the aircraft as it sees fit. The ability to seize collateral out of a bankrupt estate does not exist for any other creditor or any other asset. It is this exception to the code that forms the crux of the bondholders' leverage: pay up or surrender the planes.

Until 9/11, this structural feature had not been tested. Between 1994, when TWA filed for bankruptcy, and 2001, airline failures were limited to small, regional companies that had never issued EETCs. It was assumed that the mere presence of the section 1110 threat would heavily incentivize an insolvent airline to continue to perform all its obligations under EETC bonds. And if every so often, a plane was surrendered, how risky or complicated could it be to dispose of it without a loss?

9/11 turned this assumption on its head. The entire U.S. airline industry was teetering on insolvency, and hundreds of airplanes were idled because of the drop in air travel. Four hundred used planes were parked in the Mojave Desert airport, about ninety miles from Los Angeles. Plane prices cratered, some by 40 percent. Airlines started lining up to file for bankruptcy like passengers queue up for boarding. The first was US Airways, then in 2002 United Airlines, which had been an active issuer of EETCs, followed a few years later by Delta and Northwest.

United's bankruptcy launched an aircraft avalanche. One hundred seventy-five planes among its total fleet of four hundred sixty were being leased via securitization bonds and could conceivably come on to the market for resale or release. Bondholders *did* have the legal right to repossess their assets, but now they weren't so sure they *wanted* to. The legal advantage and financial power had slipped out of the aircraft financiers' hands.

We were in uncharted territory, with a new capital market instrument that was still untried in a downside scenario, and buyers who had been attracted to its safety and its investment-grade rating and lacked the mandate or expertise in distressed investing. Original investors had bought a supposedly bulletproof bond. They had paid one hundred cents on the dollar and woke up after 9/11 to see it trade at eighty, sixty, forty, or twenty cents. It was garbage; it was toxic. Some funds, with strategy and risk parameters that did not permit investing in junk bonds, couldn't hold on after the ratings downgrades. Some didn't have the manpower or patience to sustain the labor-intensive research required in a distressed situation. They fled the sector en masse, forcefully selling at very uneconomic prices. You don't improvise switching from trading safe, investment-grade, high-quality bonds to nonperforming junk bonds. Try asking a poet to write comics because there is a market for them. Great opportunity, wrong skill set.

Traditional credit analysis was useless at this point. What was needed was a broad view of bankruptcy and corporate restructuring, the ability to manage through a broken industry, a pile of unwanted assets, and an ill-defined road to recovery—in other words, a skillful distressed investor. Skilled or not, that is when I stepped in.

To predict the behavior of airline management teams and the performance of EETCs, the key was to understand the collateral value and legal process. The bonds were secured by aircraft, of course, but exactly what? What model, year, engine, interior configuration, flying route, maintenance record, lease rate, market value, liquidity, salability? I consulted with appraisers and brokers to discover what was trading in the aircraft market. I built my own database of lease rates and market values for each type of aircraft I encountered. I established a network of specialized traders to source bonds. I worked with tax advisors to understand and construct the optimal structure to hold the bonds.

Distressed investing takes time, and legal battles are mentally grinding. An average Chapter 11 bankruptcy case takes a year; many take two or three, after many months of preparation to file in court. A reorganization, a turnaround, or a recapitalization can have fits and starts for months or even years before reaching a consensual deal and being consummated. They require daily active involvement. You not only have to think of a winning strategy, you have to negotiate it and execute it while fending off other parties whose interests may not be aligned with yours. United, believed then to be the second-longest bankruptcy case ever, lingered in insolvency for *1,150 days*. For the better part of these three and a half years, I held interminably long weekly, often biweekly, conference calls with creditors' committees, restructuring advisors, airline consultants, and bankruptcy and litigation lawyers. United was an exceptionally aggressive debtor. The company immediately grasped the conundrum facing bondholders: the soft market for used planes and the company's own scale gave it tremendous leverage to renegotiate plane rents. Although section 1110 established that United should pay the original contract rate or give up its planes, the company did neither. Instead, it sued bondholders for antitrust violation, claiming they had colluded with one another with respect to the terms under which they would agree to continue to rent aircraft to United. The airline sought and obtained an injunction, inflicting a stunning wound to creditors—and that included me. Understand, this meant that United could use the leased planes—my planes!— without paying rent to bondholders or agreeing to return them, in essence, commit grand theft, if you ask me. And this was for an indefinite period since the bankruptcy court refused to reconvene a hearing. We fought for over two years, concurrently negotiating with United for a compromise, seeking to overturn the injunction decision in a court of appeals, and exploring alternative potential monetization of our planes. Finally, in 2005, a court of appeals reversed the lower court's decision, found the antitrust claim "thin to the point of invisibility," and handed bondholders a conclusive victory. I pocketed a handsome profit.

I had won.

There were obviously hiccups along the way. One early issue almost brought me to tears. In the office. In front of the CFO. Generally, I am not a crier. *Titanic* left me completely dry. At most, I winced at the music. For background, a hedge fund is usually domiciled in a tax-free jurisdiction, and protecting this status is of the utmost importance to profitability. It turned out that repossessing and re-leasing a plane that was once rented by a now-defunct airline could be construed as having a business in the U.S. and thus subject our fund to U.S. taxes. The CFO, a very affable, highly competent man, called me into his office to explain a troubling conundrum: the tax-free status of a hedge fund did not allow for my carefully set up, meticulously planned, and potentially lucrative restructuring. Just a decade-old careful tax construction that I was obnoxiously ignorant of. He was calm and factual. He was not deploring, just informing. There was a wrinkle, and I had no idea how to deal with it, as taxes are a foreign language to me. I feared that tears would be forming any minute until I vaguely heard the words "blocker corporation." There was a solution available, a pass-through C corporation through which the investment would have to be restructured, which he proposed to explain to me and put in place. I considered hugging him.

"You must do me this honor," I said when he finished, "that you will never give up no matter what happens, no matter how hopeless. Promise me now, and never let go of that promise. Never let go."

Just kidding. That's Jack speaking to Rose in the last scene. I was so ungrateful that I didn't even change my last name to his.

By the time United emerged from bankruptcy in 2005, we had accumulated a large portfolio of very profitable EETCs and I had extended my expertise to many other airline securities (loans, convertible bonds, municipal bonds). I pretty much knew every move in the trading playbook. One partner used to joke that when getting on a plane, I recognized the tail number and the bond it secured, a jest that I absolutely cherished. I am easily flattered.

More importantly, as United exited bankruptcy, Delta Air Lines and Northwest Airlines were getting close to filing in their turn—providing me with another batch of fantastic investment opportunities and establishing a truly enduring business line for Canyon beyond just one bankruptcy case.

Aircraft securitization could be effectively marketed to investors as an asset class that was uncorrelated to the market, meaning we could make a profit (or a loss) irrespective of the direction of the market. Of course, the goal of a hedge fund, its sole reason to exist and charge exorbitant fees, is precisely to produce profit at every turn, whether the market—stock market, bond market, loan market, what have you—goes up or down. That was the original idea, anyway, the "hedge" in hedge fund. If investors are content to collect the market return, they can buy an index or a mutual fund at a fraction of the hedge fund cost.

In the beginning, my securitization bonds were obviously correlated to 9/11, which had caused a large market decline and the bankruptcy of virtually every U.S. airline. However, in the long term, they were demonstrably uncorrelated because the fate of the bonds (and the ability to make a return) hinged on a deep understanding of the collateral and the structure and nuances of the indenture. Whether the plane could be repossessed in a bankruptcy, re-leased, or parted out for metal value, whether the bond was junior or senior, had a liquidity lending line, a buyout option... none of it had any relationship to the direction of the market and I could prove it statistically as my body of research increased.

It was a multiple win. First, aircraft securitization became a large and highly profitable part of my portfolio and Canyon's investment strategy. Second, the partners gained absolute confidence in my judgement and trading calls in the sector—my sole judgement and no one else's. I had taken the first step toward becoming a portfolio manager. Finally, the product had gained exposure with outside investors, propelling me into a key role in Canyon's front office. It meant, in essence, that my professional standing and authority had vastly improved in every respect.

CHAPTER 7

THE INDUSTRIAL AGE

2003 to 2007 marked a period of explosive growth for the hedge fund industry. The steep part of the S curve saw industry assets grow from $500 billion in the first quarter of 2003 to $2.3 trillion at the end of 2007, almost quintupling its size in a trivial five years. One can point to two main reasons, the less likely one being a steady decline in interest rates by historical standards. The ten-year Treasury yield dipped to 3.5 percent in May 2003 and stayed below 5 percent from then to, well, forever after. But back then, it was the first time since the '60s. The ten-year Treasury yield is the most widely followed benchmark of the bond market and the risk-free rate often used to measure the relative value of high-yield and distressed bonds. The riskier the bond, the greater premium investors will demand over the Treasury rate of equivalent maturity. As a shortcut, a bond is considered distressed when it yields a 10 percent premium to the ten-year Treasury bond. In other words, when Treasury bonds yield 5 percent, a distressed bond—because it is much riskier—yields 15 percent.

The federal funds rate, the interest rate at which depository institutions like banks and credit unions lend to each other, hovered around 1.5 percent until mid-2004, a level also unseen in the preceding forty years. This short-term interest rate is controlled and adjusted by the Fed in its meetings, eight times a year, to fulfill the dual mandate of full employment and stable prices. From the longest maturity to the shortest, all U.S. rates fell dramatically.

I say "by historical standards" because to a young investor starting today in the business, these yields would seem high. We have been living in a period of exceptionally low and tightly controlled interest rate for the last ten years, and it would only show that said newbie lacks context and experience in anything but Facebook and Instagram.

Back then, holders of serious money felt they were not making enough dough with traditional Treasury and corporate bond investments, and almost everyone had done terribly in the stock market during the telecom crisis and the internet bubble. Well, not quite everyone. Hedge funds had not only massively outperformed the stock market in 2001 and 2002, but also persisted on posting spectacular returns in the ensuing years with an average 11.8 percent in the years 2003–2007. Distressed hedge funds did even better, returning over 15 percent on average per year, and beating the market by over 4 percent. It was only logical for traditional investors to be pushing toward the riskier edge of the investment horizon. Seeking to diversify away from the dreary bond market and sinking stock market, staid institutional investors embarked on a steady relationship with us. From a luxury product reserved for the adrenaline-driven, risk-seeking wealthy, hedge funds became a viable asset class in their own right. Institutional investors started considering hedge funds as one of the different investments that they should have—no, that they *had* to have—and pivoted en masse to "alternative asset managers," the noncontroversial and euphemistic name now all but officially used for our sector.

The second and more important impetus for the growth is that we found a powerful preacher in the person of Yale University's chief investment officer, David Swensen, who had produced returns of over 16 percent for the twenty-year period since his hiring in 1985. Swensen's book, *Pioneering Portfolio Management*, published in 2000, blew away the old techniques of efficient frontier. He advocated diversifying away from traditional asset classes (stocks and bonds) into a vast and dynamic menu of options, particularly emphasizing the importance of private equity and hedge fund strategies while de-demonizing illiquidity. Investors should focus on "relatively illiquid markets, since rewarding investments tend to reside in dark corners, not in the glare of floodlights." Swensen was not only advertising the outperformance of Yale's endowment—justifiably so until 2008, when Yale was down some 30 percent—he was actively proselytizing. Appearing on CNBC, in the *New York Times*, and in the *Wall Street Journal*, he captured the media's attention; they romantically dubbed him "Yale's $8 Billion Man"—allegedly, the extra money he had produced for the university. Swensen convinced and converted the masses to the hedge fund creed. Up until then, endowments and universities used traditional portfolio theories developed in the '50s and '60s, targeting mostly liquid investments in static buckets, such as a simple allocation of 60 percent stocks and 40 percent bonds.

Today, the model commonly used by all large endowments and foundations is the "Swensen Approach" or the "Endowment Model." Dozens of university endowments followed his recommendation, resulting in a huge growth in hedge fund assets and numbers. The average endowment allocated about 10 percent of its assets to alternative managers in 2001. By 2007, it had roughly doubled. The biggest universities today continue to invest more than 20 percent of their assets into nontraditional areas. If Newcomen's steam engine pushed through the First Industrial Revolution and

Edison heralded the Second, then David Swensen sparked the Hedge Fund Revolution with his Endowment Model. The industry embarked on an unprecedented era of expansion in number, strategies, geographies, and assets, gleefully responding to the newly created demand with oodles of new funds at often steeply higher costs. And the money, the fees, the profit…they came pouring in. I, for one, formally express my gratitude to Mr. Swensen for giving me a career and making me rich.

A FORK IN THE ROADSHOW

As capital flooded in torrentially to our asset class, propelling hedge fund assets to $2.3 trillion by the last quarter of 2007, distressed hedge funds did even better, ballooning thirteen times in size to $324 billion. What was once a small subset of the business, amounting to 6.5 percent of all hedge fund investments in 2001, became one of the biggest, at 17.2 percent by the time of the 2008 crisis.

Canyon's growth was similarly exponential, from around $2 billion in 2001 to $10 billion in 2008 and today's roughly $25 billion. We were hardly the only ones. Almost a mirror image, Citadel (Ken Griffin's hedge fund) was running $2 billion in 2000, $12.5 billion by 2005 and around $30 billion today. The era of mass market and mass production had come to the hedge fund industry, manifesting itself not only in terms of assets under management by existing funds, but in the proliferation of new funds. They cropped up like Model Ts from a factory line, from 3,873 funds in 2000 to 8,661 in 2005.

Copycats, using me-too strategies, sprung up at an unheralded rate, as almost every legendary hedge fund gave birth to a string of new ones. From Julian Robertson's Tiger Fund (which closed in 2000) alone came thirty-eight new hedge funds by 2009, dubbed the Tiger Cubs. Young guys were leaving established hedge funds to start their own, sometimes with only a few years of experience, thinking the sky was the limit. And it did appear to be that way as assets under management between 2003 and the peak in 2008 grew at a 7.5 percent compound growth rate *per quarter*.

There is a technical term for this phenomenon in investment parlance: a crowded trade. Ironically, the great evangelist of the hedge fund trade, Mr. Swensen himself, had warned against this very danger, offering in 2007 in an interview to the *New York Times* "If you make money personally by gathering a huge pile of assets, it is great for the management company because they make bigger fees. But if the fund goes from $2 billion or $3 billion to $20 billion, they are inevitably going to reduce their ability to generate investment returns. Size is the enemy of performance." Here is the story, in a nutshell. The hedge fund industry did great as a small business, prompting a crowding out of the sector, which killed outperformance. However, Swensen's followers seemed to have missed the memo, continuing to pile on, paying the same or even higher fees to swelling funds and expecting the same persistent, outsized net returns. Past 2007, they never came back.

With the advent of the industrialization age came a divergent version of the marketing story. The original elevator pitch was that hedge funds used their small size relative to the plethora of opportunities to swoop in and capitalize on market inefficiencies, quickly getting in and out of positions. As funds became larger, the pitch morphed into the opposite story. We had access to differentiated sources of inefficiencies *because of our size*. Direct lending and rescue financing, complex financial securities like mortgage securitizations and credit default swaps, large scale bankruptcy situations like Enron and WorldCom, and later Lehman Brothers and Puerto Rico, *required* large teams of investment analysts, extensive back office and compliance departments, external financial and restructuring advisors, not to mention corporate, bankruptcy, and litigation lawyers.

It is true that some hedge fund strategies, including distressed investing, can require scale. Unless a fund owns several hundred million dollars' worth of bonds of Lehman or Puerto Rico or Caesars Palace, it has no competitive edge. It won't be part of the steering committee; it can neither influence the negotiations nor construct lucrative solutions to benefit its position. It's a passenger on the trade ride; it isn't the driver—and only spin masters can appear to make it so. However, having the edge in certain large bankruptcies comes at a heavy and *permanent* cost: illiquidity, irreversibility, stodginess, and inertia.

A FOOT IN THE DOOR

Inside the world of hedge funds, it was a period of sheer exuberance. We delivered outstanding returns and the cash kept on coming. People made more money per year than they could ever imagine, until the next year. We were reminded of F. Scott Fitzgerald, who observed, "It was borrowed time anyhow—the whole upper tenth of a nation living with the insouciance of grand dukes and the casualness of chorus girls." Well, those of us who read books were reminded, anyway.

I got my share of the bounty. Announcing my bonus to my parents became a yearly exercise in heart attack prevention. The first year, I was proud. Every year after that, they would ask, not because they cared about wealth, per se, but because they, like virtually every human walking the planet, thought the number was a gauge of success. The money was the gold star, the top school grade, the cum laude diploma.

Money wasn't my primary motivation, but it didn't hurt too much, and it certainly was how we kept score. A crass concept indeed to value one's worth in dollars—but hardly unique to the hedge fund world. Besides, I find the idea that one can make it through gumption very democratic, very "fair." To think that I, a woman, a Frenchie for whom English is a second language, could strike gold and create tangible wealth without an illustrious name, a network or connections...there is something positive and constructive in that tale. I am not sure the opportunity would have been there in France and it sure is getting rarer to come by in the U.S. I've previously, and no doubt convincingly, highlighted the death of the American Dream forty years ago. I have deplored the vanishing opportunity to rise in socioeconomic status, particularly for disadvantaged groups. Well, here is the thing, and you will not hear it from Elizabeth Warren. Wall Street is still a place, one of the few in fact in the American corporate world today, where social mobility is possible.

In that world, using one's abilities and talents can still produce an explosive rise in status. George Soros escaped Nazism in Budapest and immigrated to the UK, where he held a variety of jobs including railway porter and waiter, to finance his education. Phil Falcone of Harbinger Capital grew up one of nine children in a rather poor family in Minnesota. Leon Cooperman, founder of the legendary Omega Advisors, was the son of a plumber and the first in his family to graduate from college. Lloyd Blankfein, the famed CEO of Goldman Sachs for over a decade, came from a housing project in Brooklyn. All fulfilled multibillionaires today. If you got your foot in the door, and you were smart, you could expect more than a good living from a hedge fund job. You could make a killing. You just had to get in; that was the tough part.

MORNING BOURBON

As Canyon grew, we beefed up the staff. In 2006, we added three analysts. The year after, four more analysts and an equity trader joined the team. The year after that, the firm hired seven analysts and a bond trader. The investment team had more than doubled in three years. Until then, my title was analyst. We were all analysts except the head of research and, of course, the founding partners. It made no difference; the job, by and large, remained the same for almost a decade: to investigate potential investments and recommend trades. If you could sell the idea to the partners, you could execute the trade. The better the trade, the more capital you had at your disposal, and the more profit you stood to make. The more profit you made, the bigger the bonus received—no title needed or required. I never asked for a better one. It was a flat organization, fast, nimble, transparent, with little or no political maneuvering.

If we bought simple, liquid instruments like stocks or bonds, particularly if they traded on an exchange, the then-small back office took care of the booking and accounting. If it was a complicated, off-the-run investment, a leveraged loan or an aircraft securitization bond, then the analyst and trader rolled up their sleeves and negotiated reps and warranties with the help of an outside legal advisor, calculated accrued interest, faxed the documents to the counterparty, and made sure the closing date was respected. The grunt work took some time, for sure, and was not particularly highbrow, but it was essential to understand the nitty-gritty of the process and vocabulary of the hedge fund world. Over time, the back office staffed up. They took the administrative part of the work off an analyst's hands, but they also added a layer between the analyst and the physical realities of conducting business, the scrappiness of a trade. The investor relations team morphed into a new group: marketing. It grew like Jack's beanstalk. With an ever-increasing pool of investors with various degrees of sophistication, reporting requirements, and investing profiles, we needed a department to handhold, excuse me, deal with clients. Call me paranoid, but I swear I could not keep a secretary for more than a couple of years from 2003 to 2008. They would invariably leave me to join the marketing group as analysts, a transition that I often questioned. They were like athletes from the Soviet Union in the '80s, entering the Olympic Games just to defect to another country. If I had any qualms about my ability to manage people, this systematic poaching didn't help any.

As we added bodies in the investment group as well, members organized into teams under the supervision of a managing director or team leader and covered specific sectors, assets, and geographies. At the senior level, competition was no longer constrained to capital; it expanded to fighting for the best junior analysts (and keeping them), and for time in front of the partners to pitch trade ideas. As assets under management ballooned, so did the number of investments and complexity of our portfolio—and our business. Reporting, monitoring, and systematizing started to creep up everywhere.

I led, you guessed it, Team Mielle, which had exactly one team member in 2006, a talented young analyst whom I recruited out of Goldman Sachs.

I never dreamt of managing people. I fondly recall a class at Stanford called Interpersonal Dynamics, familiarly known as Touchy Feely, that is in such demand that a student must prioritize it above all others in order to attend. According to the school website, "Interpersonal Dynamics has been voted the most popular elective for 45 years running at Stanford GSB. For years, this course has been transforming the lives of our students, helping them unlock their true leadership potential." Its goal is to help create productive and powerful professional relationships. Like so many others, I attended the class. I mean I attended the *first* class.

We were asked to form small groups and assigned team-building exercises, the kind that are supposed to help when putting together an expedition to climb Mount Everest or something. If you're serious at all, you'll want to know: how do I really trust this fellow to hike up in the death zone when he shook my hand rather gingerly and didn't quite grasp that my name doesn't sound like "smiley"?

That's when it hit me. I would not be returning. Students said that the key to an A grade was to cry at the end of the quarter, a powerful indication of opening up to others. I would have flunked had I not quit. My tears typically come in two varieties, anger or frustration, and they are not an opening to anything except venting. To this day, my husband will attribute a mere trifle of my irritation to flunking the course.

"Should have taken Touchy Feely," he will say with a smirk and shake of his head. "My wife flunked Touchy Feely," he will freely volunteer to the cable guy who shows up outside the ten-hour window of his intervention, can't fix my TV, and is surprised to find a pinch of exasperation in my voice.

Let me add that these moments of impatience are rare, and, in my opinion, stem from legitimate reasons to lose one's mind, such as dealing with incompetence or absurdity, having to repeat oneself, being told what one already knows, or waiting.

I assume that my first analyst had grave moments of doubt about my leadership. He never showed any sign of it. I have an immense respect for his intellect, his poise, and his dry sense of humor.

"The two most important women in my life," he once declared, "are my mother and Dominique." I understand he married—but, always a loyal fellow, only after I left the firm and for all practical purposes quit his life.

One of the first investments we worked together on was Air Canada. The company had filed for bankruptcy in 2003 and emerged as a new entity called ACE a year after, with a handful of legacy businesses, including Air Canada, the flagship airline; Jazz, a domestic regional airline; ACTS, an aircraft maintenance and service group; and Aeroplan, the loyalty program. The company's valuation was allegedly lower than that of its separate components, a phenomenon that is not atypical for a public company with a complex structure. It has motivated a phenomenally successful type of hedge fund: activist investors. If the sum of the parts, in their estimation, is greater than the whole, activists will force management to split the company. In ACE's case, management was proactively seeking to disassemble the pieces, starting by spinning off Aeroplan in 2005, then moving on to Jazz airlines. Have I mentioned that nothing is ever new on Wall Street? In 2020, gravely hit by the coronavirus pandemic, cash flow-bleeding airlines around the world raced to raise money in the capital markets and borrowed from the government. Mileage programs became, once again, a source of value once forgotten and unneeded as a distinct asset from the business of flying. Not anymore. In June 2020, United, American, and Spirit Airlines mortgaged their loyalty schemes as collateral for new debt. In September, Delta Air Lines followed suit, as well as Avianca, the Colombian flagship airline which filed for Chapter 11 in May 2020 and used the value of LifeMiles as part of the collateral for its bankruptcy financing.

In any case, back then my entire team, which is to say the analyst and I, boarded a six o'clock flight one morning to Toronto to meet the management team and determine if the demerging transaction would unlock some equity value.

From time to time, I have bouts of claustrophobia and anxiety on planes, and such was the case that morning. It's no big deal, really, nothing that a glass of bourbon will not solve. I fell into a profound torpor, woke up happy upon landing, and we made our way to the meeting. In the car, the analyst asked casually if everything was OK. Splendid, I answered, confused by the question.

One can only imagine what must have gone through his head, witnessing his new boss gulping down hard alcohol at six in the morning before a business meeting, then passing out for the entire flight time (maybe drooling, snoring even).

"Dear Diary, guess what? My team leader is an alcoholic," he probably wrote that night.

I acquired some managerial skills over time, if I do say so myself—I doubt anyone else would volunteer to say so—to the great benefit of the analysts who subsequently joined him. My team grew to four members as I added more industry coverage over the next six years, and then jumped to eight as I started leading our collateralized loan obligation (CLO) business in 2012. I am enormously proud that they have now been successful hedge fund investors for over a decade. I would not say that I learned to enjoy managing a team—only that I learned to live with it as part of the job and the reality of rising in seniority.

Are there differences between a male and a female boss? I can emphatically say yes and name one for almost certain. In 2004, the Department of Justice brought an extraordinary civil lawsuit against U.S. cigarette manufacturers. Not only did the government endeavor to recoup the unfathomable sum of $280 billion, they were suing under the Racketeer Influenced and Corrupt Organizations Act, or RICO, which was originally intended to attack organized crime like the mafia. Never had it applied to corporate America. The rationale from the Clinton administration was that Big Tobacco had enjoyed profits wrongfully obtained from a lifelong marketing campaign of lies and deceit. They sought an injunction to employ these profits in the future; in practice, they asked the court to compel Big Tobacco to disgorge all profits earned from 1954 on. It had the potential to bankrupt Phillip Morris; the stock and the bonds collapsed.

I took a different view. Although I agreed that cigarette manufacturers had misled consumers, I did not believe the legal remedy was the disgorgement of profit, which meant one thing, that the bonds and stocks were a bargain. We built a large position. The trial lasted two years—during which I lived through the twists and turns of the legal system. In 2005, a district court ruled that profit disgorgement was not an available remedy under the RICO Act—a victory, though a temporary one, since the ultimate ruling of the case was a long way away. In August 2006, the judge finally issued a final judgment in a landmark opinion of almost two thousand pages. Big Tobacco was guilty of RICO violation, but the ruling ordered only prospective remedies: prohibition of certain descriptive terms (light, low tar), corrective communications, and disclosure of marketing data. Profit was not touched. The summary headlines flashed on our Bloomberg screen—"Big Tobacco win," "Phillip Morris profit unscathed"—and here is where the case became relevant to gender. I jumped out of my seat and spontaneously gave my analyst a hug and a double kiss. I don't imagine George Soros kissed his trader when he brought the Bank of England to its knees. (I do not know that for sure, though.)

Now, if you were looking for some dissertation on leadership and gender, some elaborate essay on male versus female management style, then you have the wrong book. You will need to turn to someone who enjoys pontificating. The only further thought I have on the matter is this: nothing is ever new on Wall Street. I was amused to read a few months ago that a teenager filed a RICO suit against JUUL and Philip Morris, arguing that the companies illegally marketed their e-cigarette devices to minors and lied to consumers about the health risks of vaping.

The other day I was trying to remember all the ways I invested in tobacco and I ended up sounding like Forrest Gump's "best good friend" Bubba, the shrimping boat captain. I traded in tobacco risk arbitrage, tobacco spinoffs, tobacco securitization bonds, tobacco high-yield bonds, tobacco equity, tobacco convertible bonds, tobacco manufacturers, and tobacco leaf producers. I realize that investing in tobacco is not socially responsible. I have no excuse for it and I won't attempt a joke about the French smoking (it's true; we smoke more than we wash). All I saw at the time were profit opportunities, and the tobacco sector provided me with some of my most successful and enduringly profitable trades. But self-flagellation was not my point, however deserved. I imagine that low employee turnover is helpful to most businesses; for hedge funds that invest in different strategies and throughout the life cycle of companies—growing, acquisitive, maturing, stressed and distressed, bankrupt and re-emerging—it is capital. An analyst who possesses historical and contextual knowledge of a corporation is akin to a chess master. Having memorized typical overtures, advances, and defenses, they can better recognize patterns and strategies, anticipate the next moves and, ultimately, win the game—or mitigate the loss.

You would be surprised at how many companies appeared recurrently in my portfolio. My first investment in J.Crew, the apparel company, occurred in 2004 through a private bond structured by Canyon, shortly after Mickey Drexler had joined as CEO to turn around the company, which was mostly a catalog business. Mickey had identified Madewell as a moribund brand name that he could revive under the J.Crew umbrella. He was fresh from being ousted from the Gap, which itself was experiencing growing pains, and Drexler bitterly pronounced, during our due diligence meetings, that the chain, with several thousand stores and multiple brands, suffered from overexpansion. J.Crew was much smaller. In 2006, my bonds were successfully repaid when J.Crew went public, and I reaped an extra profit by "flipping" the new equity and bonds (which means buying at the inception and selling a few days later for a small margin). In 2011, it was time to get involved in the leveraged buyout, this time through the bank debt, when the private equity funds of TPG and Leonard Green acquired the company. Throughout the years, we were profitably in and out of the name until 2014 when we exited for good, avoiding several years of steady decline. It seemed clear that retail was moving online, and that J.Crew had, in the words of its CEO that were still ringing in my ears, grown too big. By 2017, the company entered its distressed phase, crumbling over $2 billion of debt hardly supported by deteriorating earnings and a declining brand name. I got involved again, shortly but unprofitably this time. The most valuable brand had become Madewell rather than J.Crew, and equity holders were fighting to steal that value away from creditors. The story was heading toward an ugly end. It seemed wise to cut my losses. In 2020, the coronavirus spread to the U.S. and handed J.Crew its final blow; it filed for bankruptcy in May. I have no doubt that it will emerge, debt-free, and commence a third life under a "fresh-start accounting," the nomenclature to account for a reorganization. It will likely spin off Madewell and return to square one, a smaller corporation with a single brand and considerably fewer stores. If I were in the business, I would certainly be tempted to invest in a brand-new cycle.

So it goes for a litany of other names, from airlines to department stores and supermarkets. Sometimes they file for bankruptcy twice (Payless shoe stores, Gymboree, Brookstone, RadioShack). We called it Chapter 22, as in two times Chapter 11. Get it? Dying of laughter yet? Maybe nerdy finance humor is not your thing. Companies go through phases that resemble those of human beings because—and here is what an experienced analyst recognizes—companies *are* made of human beings, sometimes brilliant and often also fallible, egotistical, greedy, and power-hungry.

I tried my best to coach, help, protect, and promote my analysts (by which I mean that I fought like hell to get them paid) to ensure they would have a long career, for their sake and for mine because their tenure meant more profitable ideas. I remain close to several of them, and I salute them for sticking with me, getting the job done under incredibly trying circumstances sometimes, making me laugh often, and trying my patience only occasionally. But with their addition and that of a considerable staff, the job changed. The firm changed. As people piled up, so did procedures, reporting, hierarchy, bureaucracy, office politics—in short, all the trappings of a large, conventional, slow-moving market participant. In the beginning, hedge funds had a rebellious aspect to them, an anti-establishment mentality, and a certain scrappiness. We wanted to do things differently, discover new investing ways. We wanted to be original, innovators, inventors, explorers. It was about thinking creatively, outside the box.

In the industrialization age, we started mutating into the big, stodgy guys ourselves.

CHAPTER 8

SCRAPPY NO MORE

Yes, we made a lot of money. But we were delivering what we had promised, a product that beat the market consistently and uncorrelated returns that could not be obtained elsewhere. We earned it.

Or did we?

At the time, I did not fret over the fact that hedge funds made the managers rich but not so much the investors. Now, from the outside, I appreciate that there would be something rather off-putting, slightly unsavory, about a service of which value accrues to the seller rather than the buyer. There is enough data out there to calculate the annual profits produced by the hedge fund industry as a whole. In other words, aggregating all hedge funds into one imaginary giant firm, one can calculate how much profit it cumulatively produced over the years and, of the latter, the amount it retained as management and incentive fees versus the amount it distributed to investors as earned profits. The idea is not mine; I read it in the excellent book *The Hedge Fund Mirage* by Simon Lack and it got me calculating. I obtained slightly different numbers than Mr. Lack due to a different data source and because he stops his computation in 2010, while I take mine up to 2017. The conclusion is the same, nonetheless. From 1998 to 2017, hedge funds produced about $2 trillion of profit, of which they kept half. I am not teasing; half of the profit was never to be seen again by investors. Let them eat cake. That there isn't a Robespierre out there demanding managers' heads on a spike is astounding.

TALES OF EXCESS

The other day, I reread *Liar's Poker* by Michael Lewis, the story of Salomon Brothers in the '80s, detailing the feud between the head of corporate finance, John Gutfreund, and the head of sales and trading, John Meriwether. It was thirty years ago. Still a great read for the drama, but the numbers seem positively quaint. Gutfreund made $40 million from the sale of Salomon Brothers and paid himself $3 million. Three million? It sounds like Dr. Evil demanding a million-dollar ransom in *Austin Powers*. By today's standards, these numbers are off by a factor of a hundred.

The first manager to exceed an income of $1 billion in a single year was Eddie Lampert in 2004. Eddie, having bought Kmart out of bankruptcy in 2003, merged it with Sears in 2005. He proceeded to siphon most of the real estate value out from under investors over a decade, only to see the company file for bankruptcy again fifteen years later and barely escape total liquidation. Back then, he was part of *Time* magazine's list "the 100 men and women whose power, talent, or moral example is transforming our world." He was "the next Warren Buffett?"—I jest not, the question and his picture were on the cover of *Business Week* in November 2004, with the subtitle "Will he build [Kmart] into a new Berkshire Hathaway?" Today, he is the man who presided over two hundred thousand layoffs, four thousand store closures, and tens of billions of losses in one of the biggest retail failures of all time. Call me hurtful, but I would offer a resounding "no" to both questions. His hedge fund dwindled from a peak of $18 billion to $2 billion. With enough time, the market has a merciless way to judge Icarian managers. Still, he supposedly managed to hang on to a personal fortune of almost $1 billion—and he once made the cover of *Business Week*.

Before the internet and social media took off, the hedge fund business was unrivaled in terms of systematic wealth creation—for its own people. Do you believe that Wall Street bankers make a lot of money? It's chump change, really. Consider that in 2006, Lloyd Blankfein, the CEO of Goldman Sachs, reportedly earned $54 million. Meanwhile, the average pay of a top twenty-five hedge fund manager that year was $570 million. The top three, James Simons of Renaissance, Ken Griffin of Citadel, and Eddie Lampert of ESL, made over $1 billion each. A senior portfolio manager made ten times the bonus of an investment banker with similar tenure. Now, recognize that often, a large part of this is not distributed income. At Canyon, as in most hedge funds, a hefty portion of our bonus was not handed out in cash, but rather mandatorily reinvested in our own fund. Although it does not apply to the support staff and the back office, every hedge fund professional above a certain amount of earnings sees an increasing percentage (30 percent to 50 percent) of their bonus locked up for years in their fund. Putting your proverbial money where your mouth is acts as a powerful incentive for managers to perform and rightfully aligns your interests with those of the investors. That is the idea, anyway, and it works to a point—the point at which the fund becomes large enough that management fees are bigger than performance fees. By 2007, we were dangerously close to it.

LEO'S FRIEND

Some investors pride themselves on not having a lavish lifestyle. I can name one. It must be lonely. Warren Buffett has over a fifty-year-long, carefully polished image of being down to earth. For the rest of us, not so much.

When money came, I turned out to be as much of a jackass as the best hedge fund guy out there. Did I ever long for a diamond ring? Not really. I once delivered a righteous speech about De Beers artificially inflating diamond prices by controlling supply to my then-boyfriend (now husband). Besides, every woman wore a diamond solitaire—what an unoriginal sign of commitment. And who needed a sign that would provide no protection to a marriage should times of trouble emerge? A prenup, maybe. A diamond ring, why? Yet a diamond ring we bought in 1999, in the jewelry district of downtown Los Angeles, a small stone but of excellent quality, my husband hastens to add. By 2005, when asked what I wished for our fifth wedding anniversary, I naturally suggested a bigger diamond. "You want to get rid of your engagement ring?" my husband asked, dismayed. "Of course not," I said, "Not get rid of. Trade it."

I confess, I am not sentimental about objects. I have no understanding of why people keep things. I suffer from compulsive decluttering disorder. The fact that the American Psychiatric Association has not recognized it as a mental condition is regrettable. It would have helped explaining to my children that I invariably trashed their Mother's Day gifts, be it a papier-mâché bouquet of flowers, a fingerprint-painted flowerpot, or a frame decorated with dry pasta. I once managed to toss the license plates that had come in the mail for our brand-new and temporarily registered car. It is a serious condition that I would invoke as an attenuating circumstance for acquiring a second diamond ring.

In 2006, my bonus hit seven numbers and it was time for ring version 3.0. Then, I really had no excuse. I know that external signs of wealth are classless and crass. Any casual anthropological study would show that flashy diamonds and head-to-toe luxury-brand outfits add thirty pounds to a woman's ass; that a Bentley, a Rolls, or a Jaguar highlights a man's emerging baldness; that a ten-thousand-square-foot mansion makes the owner look puny and inadequate.

I felt deeply guilty. Nonetheless, there we went, trundling off to visit Martin Katz jewelry in Beverly Hills, seeking to flash my success with an ostentatious symbol. Katz is known as the jewelry purveyor to the stars. I read that he bejeweled a pair of Ray-Ban sunglasses for Celine Dion by encrusting them with diamonds. My French friends would be mortified, even if Celine does sing in French sometimes. The new ring was a 2.5-carat rose-cut diamond with a micro-diamond band. I proudly wore it as I boarded a flight to a meeting in New York. On the plane, I watched the excellent new release *Blood Diamond*. I stared at the ring. I looked around me. Had anyone spotted my finger and then logically and accurately connected me with the revolting child-soldier creators, civil-war perpetrators, African country-abusers from the movie? I drove right back to the store and asked Martin himself if he could legally trace the diamond. He assured me that he could, going on to note that he had seen *Blood Diamond* and was a friend of Leonardo DiCaprio. Was the latter information supposed to comfort me in the morality of the purchase? Leonardo is, as best as I can tell, an environmentalist, a friend of the earth, and an exceptionally beautiful human being. How could I doubt that purchasing a ring from a friend of his was anything but just? I kept the bloody thing for about ten years, wearing it less and less. I ended up trading it too, this time for cash at a pawn shop. In a karmic sign of justice and fairness, I lost a third of its cost in the process.

THE FRENCH MOTTO

The problem with rich people is not that they are different, contrary to what Fitzgerald so eloquently proposed, and it is not just that they have more money, as Hemingway responded. The problem with rich people is that there is no constraint on their stupid ideas. Most of us have dumb ideas on a regular basis, but either we don't have the means to implement them, or someone tells us they are stupid, or both. Maybe you thought that it would be neat to, say, take heavy doses of Propofol and sleep in an oxygen tent while your pet chimpanzee jumps around the bed. Or it'd be nifty to own a twenty-bedroom home for your family of four with a dedicated gift-wrapping space and a wraparound river with dolphins. Then you remembered you should first pay the kids' school tuition, or a friend pronounced you a raving lunatic, and it all stayed at a rather exploratory stage.

When the mega-rich have mega-dumb ideas, however, they go through unbridled. The check-and-balance system of absurdity no longer applies. The sushi-loving hedge fund foodie orders the entire menu for dinner because he just cannot decide. The hedge fund party-lover invites guests at an all-night soiree to vandalize with spray paint his $52 million Manhattan penthouse because it is soon to be remodeled. Yet another purchases a six-thousand-acre estate in Maryland that includes three islands shaped into his initials, PTJ, for Paul Tudor Jones, because, well, he owns them. All capital ideas.

In the category of nothing is ever new, this sort of deplorable behavior has happened before. I just spent three weeks in Brazil, and the city of Manaus struck a particular chord. Born out of absolutely nothing, in the heart of the Amazon, the city developed into one of the largest, wealthiest cities in the world in the nineteenth century following the discovery of the rubber tree. Rubber and latex became a revolutionary material for European industries.

Entrepreneurial adventurers from all over Europe, the "rubber barons," flocked to the city and made extravagant fortunes. The peak period lasted thirty years, from 1890 to 1920. "No extravagance, however absurd, deterred the rubber barons. If one rubber baron bought a vast yacht, another would install a tame lion in his villa and a third would water his horse with champagne."[6]

That will surely give some of my former colleagues a few ideas. Hold on thanking me because here is the foreboding end of the story. By the beginning of the twentieth century, rubber seeds were smuggled and trees transplanted to Malaysia, where production became cheaper and more efficient. The British Empire seized control of the market; the Brazilian monopoly ended abruptly and so did the rubber boom. Manaus fell into poverty. Rubber plantations closed, mansions were sold or given to the local administration, and entrepreneurs packed up and left, many having lost their fortune and more than one declaring bankruptcy. It is intellectually pleasing, is it not, to put in parallel the golden age of the rubber industry with that of the hedge fund?

As for myself, maybe I was not rich enough to completely lose touch with reality. Or just call me patriotic: Liberté, Egalité, Fraternité, which loosely translates to "Flaunt Not Your Money." Despite almost thirty years in the U.S., I can't shake my French essence. What I eat, what I wear, what interests me, and how I judge people all bear the indelible stamp of my country of origin. I place a high importance on how people present themselves, their sense of style, and their attractiveness. I value protocols and etiquette, particularly table manners and chivalry, rare commodities in finance. I never got used to having a meal with some American male colleagues. Their idea of sophistication was to be childishly specific or crassly picky. Can you cut the sushi in six instead of four pieces? Is there salt in the chicken? Dressing on the salad? Potatoes in the fries? Or, I only eat grain and anchovies. No fish and seafood except lobster frittata with caviar fuzz. The way they hold the fork—are we eating a steak or cavemen hunting? Should a knife or a finger reach into the mouth for some exquisitely elaborate forensic exploration? Please, don't answer that. I have explained tricky investment ideas to a coworker who was flossing. I have led a meeting where a trader was cutting his nails. I have witnessed a colleague keep his headset screwed on his skull while going to the toilet, talking as he went in and back out again. One day, as I was changing into my workout clothes in one of the two gender-neutral bathrooms of the office gym, I heard a conversation so clearly it sounded like it was next door. Because it was. When I came out, an analyst was standing by the adjacent restroom, listening to the COO talk through the closed door. I raised an eyebrow at the unlucky fellow. Seriously? He diplomatically cut off the exchange with the news that Dominique was about to jump on the treadmill and perhaps they should reconvene at a later time and different place. Why, here is a daring statement: no one is so indispensable that they should not postpone a conversation to go to the commode.

As a Frenchwoman, I am more impressed by culturally literate people than wealthy ones—and by culture, I mean literature, classical music, and fine art. I once asked a colleague if he liked opera and was bemused by his answer. "She's OK," he said. After I made clear that I didn't mean Oprah the media mogul but the thingy with big people singing in a theater, he added, "I like folk music," as if that were a comparison or a compensation. Familiar territory at last. Bela Bartok's *Romanian Folk Dances*, Marquez's *Danzon*, Copland's *Appalachian Spring*! Emboldened, I threw in a little controversial jest about Tchaikovsky's "Russian Song" because, why not, we were now on solid common ground. Many hedge fund managers I have met have never set a foot in a museum save for a charity dinner, or a concert hall save for serving as a board member. They wouldn't recognize Caravaggio if he painted their private plane or Bach if he played for their Peloton class. In other words, I am a French snob.

Not to generalize, but I do believe John Lennon was referring to men on Wall Street when he sang that they think themselves so clever and class-free but are still peasants as far as the eyes can see.

THE TIPPING POINT

When I started, people around me genuinely loved the market, the game, trading, the adrenaline, and the competition. They were passionate about finance, profoundly creative, original, and intellectually curious. The partners at Canyon were wickedly smart, intense, and eminently quirky. My job interview had a decidedly different feel than at Morgan Stanley or Goldman Sachs. Canyon was a small venture and they wanted—no, they needed—to make it. There was a sense of urgency, of immediacy, of now-or-never energy. Every decision is live or die in the early stage of a hedge fund—a few months of poor performance and *poof!* you're closing shop. Within half a decade, it all changed, and hedge fund founders became captains of industry.

By 2007, the cat was out of the bag. Kitson, a hip store in West Hollywood, was selling T-shirts that read, "Kiss me, I'm a hedge fund SOB." With time, scale, and size, the scrappiness disappeared, and for me, the joyous sense of adventure went with it. Legitimacy undermined the strength of the hedge fund business by introducing some level of conservatism. It chilled the spirits of the adventurers, those intrepid traders going out West looking for new ways to make money. We had arrived at a city long settled. With legitimization also came the escalating expenses of an ever-growing organization. I mentioned already that our investment team expanded, and that our marketing team literally ballooned. The costs piled on; a larger pool of investors requires larger customer relations, compliance, legal, IT, and accounting departments.

But the real killer is that size is the enemy of performance. Don't take my or David Swensen's word for it. In an entertaining 1995 shareholder letter, Warren Buffett defined the conundrum of investment success. "The giant disadvantage we face is size: In the early years, we needed only good ideas, but now we need good big ideas. Unfortunately, the difficulty of finding these grows in direct proportion to our financial success, a problem that increasingly erodes our strengths." Numerous academic studies show that emerging fund managers perform better than established ones for a plethora of reasons, but Buffett captured it all in two sentences.

My experience is that it is hard enough to have ten solid ideas every year. When you invest $20 billion, you don't need ten but a hundred. A hundred original, profitable, executable ideas when ten thousand funds are competing for the same edge is a tall order. Why not invest $1 billion in twenty good ideas, you cleverly ponder, rather than $200 million in a hundred? Because not every idea can sustain that investment size—many markets, financial instruments, corporations, and restructurings are too small and too illiquid. You would move the price by investing that much. You sacrifice trading speed, agility, nimbleness, and reversibility, which are intrinsic to good ideas to begin with. You are scrappy no more.

GOODBYE TO 90210

To be fair, the very first telltale sign of the new era happened years before. Wearing jeans in the office suddenly became unacceptable except on Fridays. We needed to dress in business attire because one, what do you know, we were a business, and two, we had exponentially more investors visiting the office and expecting a sartorially respectable workforce. The partners sent out a memo to this effect, causing widespread consternation among the young employees. A team of analysts delegated me to negotiate, which pleased me enormously. I felt rather like Lech Wałęsa, the Polish union organizer who fought against a totalitarian regime and won the Nobel Peace Prize in the '80s.

To back up a moment, truthfully, I did not wear jeans much. I love fashion and I enjoyed dressing up for the office. I often lamented that I lacked a discerning audience, however. The first time I tucked my pants into thigh-high boots on a winter day in 2005—years ahead of the legendary 2011 Hermes gaucho collection, you understand—a colleague asked where I had parked my horse. The only comment on my fabulous vintage sequined Chloe pants from 2001 (a runway cult, truly) was a deplorable, "You still fit into pants from ten years ago?" It did not faze me. I see no contradiction between looking stylish and looking serious. Neither do I find a conflict in advocating for gender parity yet welcoming gallantry. I find it absurd and undermining when women renounce their femininity in the name of equality. "Dress shabbily and they remember the dress; dress impeccably and they remember the woman," said Coco Chanel, an admirable and immensely successful businesswoman. It's all a matter of taste, of course. Mine happens to be impeccable.

So admittedly, I did not entirely grasp the jeans fuss, but a true leader rises above personal feelings and the denim cause seemed a worthy undertaking. Except that when I asked the reason for such an interdiction, the reason was somewhat undignified.

"Look, Dominique," one of the partners said, "some of our female employees wear jeans without underwear."

For context, low-rise jeans were the rage at the time. But I don't know why the issue seemed to strictly reside on women's asses and why it was deemed OK to be butt-naked on Fridays.

"Well, nothing in the new policy prevents these women from wearing other types of pants commando-style," I objected. "If that's the true complaint, why don't you change the policy from banning jeans to requiring panties?"

Pretty clever diplomacy, I reckoned, but it did not win the argument. Sadly, I had to put an end to my budding political aspirations.

We left our Beverly Hills office in 2008. We had started with half a floor, expanded to the full floor (and dislodged my dentist), then another floor, then another one. But more room did not transform the space into a particularly inspiring one for our brand-spanking-new institutional investors. The women's bathroom kept on clogging. I complained to the office manager (a woman), who complained to the building manager (a man). He empathetically urged us to use less toilet paper. It was time to leave the crap behind.

I looked around at all the packed boxes in the empty space with no small amount of emotion on the last day in the old office. We were moving to a newly built building in Century City, where CAA (Creative Artists Agency), the top Hollywood agency firm, was also relocating. Before you ask me if I saw celebrities in the elevator, let me disillusion you. They do not come to work at six in the morning. At the time, it was one of the most expensive office spaces in the city. My office was simply magnificent, with a glorious view of the ocean and spectacular sunsets. The valet parked my car every morning and fetched it at night, or as many times as I needed it during the day. We had balconies, two kitchens, non-clogging women's bathrooms, and a spacious, well-appointed gym. It is one thing when twenty people share an open office and investors do not get a bottle of water because, you know, it's an additional cost. It is quite another to support a twenty-thousand-square-foot lease and the salaries and bonuses of more than a hundred people.

Before we relocated, I toured the construction site with the COO, who sat me down for a crucial conversation. What furniture did I prefer in my office—conference table and chairs or couch and coffee table? Color of shelves? Credenza or file cabinet (was there a difference) by the window? It spooked me. I had not had an office for years. I sat in a cubicle on the trading floor. Then I shared a diminutive office with a tobacco-chewing analyst. The spitting, let alone that I could touch his desk with my toes if I indulged in extending my legs, did not affect our relationship. Quite the contrary. He is a lifelong friend and now a nonsmoking, non-spitting, perfectly respectable hedge fund fellow, if there is such a thing, of course.

I am not particularly superstitious, but surveying the luxury floor of our new abode, I had a feeling right then and there that we were cooked.

...I don't mind dying

Ritually, since I always rise again,

But I should have liked a little more blood

To show they were taking me seriously.

—U. A. FANTHORPE

"Not My Best Side"

CHAPTER 9

MURDER ON THE ORIENT EXPRESS

I am not a historian, nor am I an economist. I cannot pretend to comprehensively explain the conditions that led to the financial crisis of 2008. What I observed, however, is that it had the two ingredients of every financial crisis, plus a couple others that made it the equivalent of a capital markets Molotov cocktail.

The first two conditions that you find at the heart of virtually all asset price bubbles are leverage (too much debt) and speculation (too much greed). The Tulip mania of 1637, the first record of a speculative bubble, when prices of tulips in Holland soared and then collapsed for reasons still uncertain today; the Great Depression of 1929; Black Monday in 1987; the dot-com bubble in 2000—they all had the same root causes. One of the oldest books about Wall Street, *Reminiscences of a Stock Operator* by Edwin Lefèvre, which recounts the life of stock trader Jesse Livermore around 1890 to 1920, said it categorically a hundred years ago:

"There is nothing new on Wall Street. There can't be, because speculation is as old as the hills. Whatever happens in the stock market today has happened before and will happen again."

Flash forward to 2008. This time the tulips were houses, and everyone was in on it, from the top to the bottom of the economic chain. There were buyers who wanted to own homes they couldn't afford, mortgage lenders who extended loans to buyers they shouldn't have financed, bankers who securitized mortgages into over-leveraged bonds, insurers and rating agencies who gave phony safety ratings to said bonds, investors who recklessly relied on these ratings to speculate on home prices, and, of course, politicians who deregulated the banking industry to encourage a booming economy led by housing.

The housing bubble was the crisis ignition point, although in my opinion, *bubble* isn't the best term. A better analogy is a pendulum. When a weight suspended from a pivot swings far out in one direction, it swings back to the opposite side with a force equal to the momentum it had going in the first direction.

Housing prices weren't the only ones reaching speculative extremes; around the globe risk premia (the extra profit you earn to hold risky investments) in general had compressed to radical lows, which pushed hungry investors to go after ever more illiquid, opaque, complex investments. Innovative but complex financial investments such as mortgage securitizations, credit default swaps (a financial contract akin to an insurance policy that pays out in the case of a corporate bond default), and carry trades (where one borrows money at a low interest rate to buy an asset that should provide a higher return) ballooned.

Everyone, and I do mean everyone, was encouraged to use debt recklessly. The banking industry was permitted to leverage their balance sheets thirty-five times, meaning they could burden their capital structure with thirty-five times more debt than equity—

instead of ten times in the '70s and '80s, and twenty times in the '90s. Meanwhile, my contractor, an affable and highly competent man who can hold a long and lively conversation about cement, was allowed to borrow beyond his credit score and at one point owned seven income properties before he had to file for bankruptcy in 2009. Was there a moral responsibility that lenders not take advantage of these conditions? In addition, did that standard apply equally to the CEOs of Bear Stearns, Lehman Brothers or Merrill Lynch, who jeopardized the entire banking system, and the homeowner who fabricated the income on his loan application? Should the former be held to a higher standard?

My husband proposed this apt analogy: If you build a settlement on an earthquake fault line, and a monstrous tremor destroys the entire city, whose responsibility is it? The people who chose to live there? The developer and construction companies who built their houses? The insurance firms who offered coverage? The bankers who extended mortgage financing? The government who zoned the area as residential?

2008 was the equivalent of *Murder on the Orient Express*, and, as Hercules Poirot found, everyone was at least partially guilty of the financial bloodbath. Alan Greenspan, the Federal Reserve chairman who believed in the efficiency of markets like it was the Bible, played a special role in the unraveling. On September 14, 2007, some twenty months after stepping down as Fed chairman, he gave an interview on CNBC to Maria Bartiromo. Remember, we were then on the doorstep of one of the biggest financial blow-ups of all time. Yet Greenspan opined:

Credit default swaps have been an extraordinarily valuable tool in the sense a substantial proportion of loans that are made, are made by leveraged institutions. And in previous decades, they left those loans on their balance sheets. And when there was stress, they had a banking crisis. Or you had savings and loan crisis, or something of that nature. With the credit default swap, you have the originators of loans capable of selling off the credit risk to those with far less leverage, who are willing to accept the risk at a price. And since we've had credit default swaps, there has not been a major financial institution undermined. And I think it's been an extraordinary advance. And the way you can tell it's useful is to look at the notional values of CDS. It just has gone through the roof. There are very serious questions currently about a lot of the structured products that have gotten so sophisticated and so technical, driven and priced by internal models, as distinct from market prices, that I think in certain areas we have gone too far. The market will straighten it out. In other words, when this particular episode is over—and it will be over at some point— we're gonna find that certain products which had a terrific vogue during the period, but were found to be very difficult to price, will probably shrink in in size. They may not disappear, but their orders of magnitude will come down quite significantly.

Was anyone *paying attention to* this? Greenspan believed that the very fact that a financial instrument has grown like a weed is proof of its intrinsic worth to the system. In the same breath, he acknowledged that some instruments might be out of control in volume and complexity. But, not to worry, the market will automatically correct.

Call me finicky, but how exactly can the market both be the Great Validator and the Great Regulator? And even if it were true that the market eventually self-regulates—emphasis on *eventually*—was anyone asking, When? And at what societal cost?

Seventy thousand dollars in lifetime income for the average American—that was the societal cost of the 2008 crisis according to a study cited by Christine Lagarde, then finance minister of France (and the first woman to hold such a position in a G-7 country). I am not citing her because she went on to become chairman of the International Monetary Fund (another first for women), because I admire her sense of fashion (although I do), or because she is French (although she is), or even because as a child she was a synchronized swimmer (although I have a weak spot for incongruous hobbies). I quote her because she observed, "If it had been Lehman Sisters rather than Lehman Brothers, the world might well look different today."

Lehman filed for bankruptcy on September 15, 2008, and eventually liquidated. The crisis brought this venerable institution of close to 160 years to its knees in less than one. The Lehman failure has since been the subject of several movies, plays, and books—not mine. I'll just reiterate its seismic importance in the 2008 crisis, not only because of the size of the debacle—over $600 billion in debt, twenty-five thousand employees, offices around the world—but also because of its dire consequences on financial markets around the world.

Christine Lagarde's jest aside, the point remains. Virtually no one doubted Greenspan's gospel, although financial innovation had so vastly outgrown regulation and supervision that it had created the very eye of the storm. With 2008 a high point in Wall Street groupthink, a reckoning was inevitable. And a "key ingredient of [any future] reform would be more female leadership in finance," Lagarde has written. "First, greater diversity always sharpens thinking, reducing the potential for groupthink. Second, this diversity also leads to more prudence, with less of the reckless decision-making that provoked the crisis. Our own research bears this out—a higher share of women on the boards of banks and financial supervision agencies is associated with greater stability."

Her research is not unique. Former trader and neuroscientist John Coates argued in his 2012 book *The Hour Between Dog and Wolf* that financial bubbles could be a "young male phenomenon" due to a testosterone feedback loop in exuberant markets. Most investment teams look like a male rowing team. It's efficient for working in unison but considerably less impressive when the crew is rowing in the wrong direction. A 2014 study by six researchers from top universities and published by the National Academy of Sciences found that "bubbles are affected by ethnic homogeneity in the market and can be thwarted by diversity."[7] Alas, of the ten directors on Lehman's board in 1998, nine of them were white men. The only woman, a retired U.S. Navy admiral, had no prior finance or banking experience. This diversity wasteland was, and still is today, inherent and emblematic of the finance industry.

Add to leverage, speculation, and groupthink a last ingredient, the secret sauce of the 2008 recipe: contagion. The crisis spread wider and faster across industries and geographies than any time before. Globalization of banking and finance enabled the disease to spread around the world like a Kim Kardashian TV show. It was not just interconnectivity and correlation between markets around the globe. It was true contamination. Firms, industries, markets, and entire countries were falling sick without necessarily a direct contact with patient zero (the U.S. subprime housing market, which is the portion of the real estate market financed by mortgages to lenders with low credit scores) because fears of financial collapse led to the withdrawal of funding from financial institutions around the world on a scale never seen before.

Some studies contend that the Global Financial Crisis, as it is now known, brought forward the concept of "systemic risk." There was a clear triggering event: mounting defaults in the U.S. subprime mortgage loans. Once it hit, it prompted a domino effect, destroying mortgage securitization bonds, which had been sold to investors around the world, and engulfing the investment banks that had issued them and that still held a generous pile. Reeling from their mounting losses, the banks stopped providing funding and liquidity to each other and their financial counterparties, including hedge funds. A massive, global, endemic credit crunch ensued, which, combined with plummeting asset values, led to worldwide economic activity slowing to a grind.

A SEPTEMBER TO REMEMBER

So we found ourselves way out on a limb in underestimating and underpricing risk, and happily going about our business until such time as it could no longer be ignored. I remember the exact day that happened for me. It was Sunday, September 14, 2008. The Canyon senior managers had been invited to a beautiful party for the daughter of one of the partners. The event was held on a vast beachfront property in Malibu owned by Larry Ellison of Oracle, who has since turned it into a high-end commercial development anchored by a Nobu restaurant. It was a picture-perfect day and they had set up, as one does, multiple dance floors and bars, entertainers, dancers, white leather furniture, ice sculptures, and a splendid buffet. Hundreds of dressed-up guests with their spouses and children were determined to have a jolly time.

Except the news never stops. Financial stories roll in before and after market hours, including Sundays. No matter the day or time, a market of something is open somewhere—Asia, Europe, currency exchange, futures. Before the end of the party, an ominous headline hit the screens of our BlackBerries (this was but little more than ten years ago): Lehman Brothers to file a disorderly bankruptcy Monday morning. A bankruptcy is generally a well-planned process that a company can—no, *is expected*—to survive by optimizing its assets and reducing its debt load under the protection of the court. A "disorderly" bankruptcy is rare and extreme; it is financial chaos. George Soros later described it in rigorous medical terms. "Allowing Lehman to fail," he said, caused "a cardiac arrest of the financial system." I wondered if the party planners had arranged for defibrillators. I marveled at the ice sculpture melting away and disintegrating in the hot afternoon sun. It was exactly what the market would do on Monday.

Lehman was the liquidity provider for many funds and countless companies, a critical piece of the Wall Street maze in which all the players were hopelessly intertwined. Canyon, like every hedge fund, used Lehman as a counterparty, or a trading partner. We had not been only sitting on pending trades where we had sold them stocks, bonds and loans, but also ongoing contracts, credit and interest rate swaps, warehousing lines, you name it. So when Lehman's stock started falling, from $65 per share at the beginning of 2008 to $12 in July, and rumors of a potential insolvency could be validated by an even cursory analysis of the cash balance, it became clear that left to its own fate, Lehman would unravel. We didn't need to wait and find out if a white knight would come to the rescue, all hands were on deck. My colleague Jeff redirected our business throughout July and August, diligently unwinding the strings that connected us to Lehman, so that when they filed, we had virtually no exposure. But he pointed out that given the speed at which one investment bank after another could melt toward bankruptcy—first Bear Stearns, then Lehman, then Morgan Stanley, Merrill Lynch, and Goldman Sachs—he would run out of possible counterparties before year-end.

Still, at the beginning of September, with Lehman's stock still hanging around $10 per share, market participants firmly expected the government to step in and arrange for a hasty merger between

Lehman and a healthier financial institution, with a tidy fulfillment of its obligations to follow. I recalled Long-Term Capital in 1998, the hedge fund that was forced into a sale by the Fed to avoid a frenzied unravelling of billions of intertwined borrowings and lending around the globe. This time was different. Simply put, government officials and Wall Street bankers ran out of time—or goodwill. The simple fact that Lehman could fail—was allowed to fail—meant that *any* bank could fail. There was no safe haven anymore in investment banks or commercial banks. Panic spread throughout the financial market, even among institutions and investments with no interconnection with Lehman at all. The cornerstone of our financial system is that banks lend liberally and cheaply to each other and to financial players all over the world. When the ability to move capital suddenly and entirely dried up, a liquidity crisis of such scale and depth ensued that it ground the economy to a complete halt. No more money flowing through the veins of the planet's financial system—an economic heart attack.

Many of our hedge fund peers did not have the time or sense of foreboding to get out of their Lehman relationships. Again, most believed that the government would intervene with a rescue package in the form of loans, equity infusion, or a forced merger. Or maybe the size of their operations or pressure from Lehman itself prevented them from severing their ties. Whatever the reasons, now faced with a failed Lehman, they were out of luck. Filing for bankruptcy meant that Lehman would not, could not, fulfill its contracts and financial obligations. Its assets were frozen. If you were owed money because you had sold a bond or any other transaction, your money was held in the estate as soon as they filed for Chapter 11 and remained there until the company's emergence from bankruptcy (always years later!) or a specific order from the bankruptcy court. This is called the "bankruptcy stay." The moment a bankruptcy petition is filed, an automatic injunction halts creditors from collecting debts from the company. For creditors of Lehman Brothers, this created the mother of all cash squeezes. It was like losing a game of Jenga. Once the Lehman piece was taken away, the whole thing came crashing down.

Ten days after that ill-fated beachfront party, we held our research retreat, an annual corporate event for the investment team (traders, portfolio managers, and analysts) usually set in an off-site hotel so luxurious that we had to be locked up in a windowless conference room for eight hours a day or we could have actually enjoyed ourselves. Outside guests from the financial world made presentations on different topics with various degrees of tediousness until the third day when, driven to despondency by the monotony of some speakers and the frigid temperature of the room, we were mercifully dismissed for "team-building activities." Oh the fun of it all. One year, we climbed up what looked to me like electric poles for a tightrope-walking exercise. While waiting for their turns, our fellow colleagues below bet on which one of us dead-men-walking would fall off (thankfully, we had been given climbing harnesses, so no bets paid off). Another year we had a tandem kayaking race. They partnered me with a colleague twice my weight, if I am charitable. "I want to be in the front to direct," he commanded me at the start line. We were so forward-loaded that we flipped over. "Get in the back seat before I knock you unconscious with the paddle," I offered constructively. Nothing like it to build *esprit de corps* and camaraderie; it was a genuine bonding experience.

On September 24, 2008, we settled at the posh Four Seasons resort in Santa Barbara. Companies were collapsing at lightning speed. Lehman had filed on September 15. AIG had been taken over by the government through an $85 billion bailout on September 16, and Goldman Sachs had been thrown an equity infusion lifeline by Berkshire Hathaway on September 23. March 2008, when Bear

Stearns was sold for $2 a share to JP Morgan to avoid bankruptcy by a hair's breadth, seemed an eternity away.

Markets were generally going in the same direction around the world: tanking. After a heavy agenda on the first day, we were scheduled to dine *al fresco*. We all walked out on to the lush garden, richly landscaped and perfectly manicured, at last breathing in fresh air and enjoying the light of day. I was resolutely going after the bar and the buffet, in that order, when the news came that Washington Mutual, a deeply distressed California bank in which Canyon had invested, was holding a conference call announcing an immediate merger with JP Morgan.

Understand, we had hoped for exactly that transaction, in which the regional bank would be bought by a much larger one, shoring up its balance sheet and credit worthiness. The mood on the front lawn turned positively upbeat if not boastful, and the position managers marched back, heads high, to the conference room to listen in while the rest of us waited to uncork the champagne. An hour after, they came back. If I were a movie critic, I would place the story between *Braveheart* and *Saving Private Ryan*. The brave departure and hope for a better future, the feeling that victory is within reach, and suddenly, *wham*! Defeat and capitulation. We were still standing to fight, but we had lost a critical battle.

Washington Mutual had indeed been "bought"—for barely a dime a share, a miserable fraction of a dollar. It was not the marriage of two consenting parties. It was a shotgun wedding unceremoniously orchestrated by the Federal Reserve and the Treasury Department. The company was not simply running out of liquidity, it had too much debt, too many bad loans, and not enough time. It was running out of options and would imminently go belly-up unless someone rescued it. We lost almost every penny of our investment. At the seafood buffet, it looked like the crab legs were giving us the finger.

PANIC ATTACKS

To this day, I cannot watch or read anything that evokes the 2008 crisis without experiencing palpitations and eyebrow sweat. It was that personally traumatizing. My theretofore mild and manageable claustrophobia mushroomed into a full-grown handicap. After our retreat, I decided to get a facial at a fancy spa, thinking that some pampering might help me unwind. It all started swimmingly. I was lying on my back, the statutory cucumbers on my eyelids, scented mud on my face, and ersatz Tibetan music playing softly in the background. The aesthetician told me to relax for fifteen minutes and left the room. Within seven, I was overwhelmed by such anxiety that I could hardly breathe. I got up, blinded by the vegetables and gagging from the goop dripping over my face, took a few wobbly steps with my arms wildly stretched in front of me searching frantically for the door, and came out of the treatment room in my underwear yelling for help. A full-on lunatic. I haven't been to a spa since.

I had the same experience at the opera. The opening act of *The Flying Dutchman* triggered another episode—minus the cucumber and the public viewing of my panties. My heart began to palpitate along with those same sensations of sweating and smothering. I stepped on half a dozen people's toes and rushed out of the concert hall. And so it went. On planes, I would frantically ring the flight attendant for a drink because of sudden suffocation. I tried meditating and dutifully took a Buddhism class. I had a panic attack just sitting on the classroom floor and closing my eyes.

The truth is, I felt deeply ashamed for having lost so much money in the 2008 debacle. When you're down 25 percent, your ability to endure self-doubt is greatly compromised. I rehashed my positions and decision process in a never-ending mental loop. I lost confidence in my ability to invest and make sound judgments on the market. And the way back up wasn't easy. There was no market to speak of for junk bonds, leveraged loans, and most of our assets from mid-2008 to spring 2009. For financial securities that do not trade through an electronic stock exchange, like many corporate fixed income instruments including junk bonds and distressed securities, a trader must match an actual physical buyer and a seller, much like a real estate broker representing a house. If there is no willing seller or buyer—the seller is loath to sell at what he considers a ludicrously low bid and the buyer is unwilling to step up to what he believes is a preposterous ask—there is simply no trade at all. For months on into 2009, traders would take a trading order and never call back, or an order would linger for weeks unfulfilled. The corporate bond market was all but frozen.

As Jeff had predicted, we were running out of creditworthy partners to trade with. Yet basic decency dictated that we bravely continue to show up for our investors and to keep the business alive. A hedge fund does not get paid incentive fees until it reaches its high watermark (meaning it has recouped the money it has lost) and produces new profit. I went to work every day not being able to do anything but count my paper losses and feel terrible. Perhaps the experience was made worse by my gender. Some research[8] points to women being more fearful of failure, of experiencing shame and embarrassment or of devaluing their self-worth. But here is the great market equalizer: 99 percent of people around me were men, and they had lost just as much, if not much more, money than I. So what if they just *felt* better about it than I did? That would not help investors. In other words, my feeling was not grief but self-pity, an unattractive, unproductive state that I detest if and when I am able to recognize it. Once I do—allowing for a modicum of sadness and depression or anger and self-loathing—I move on to my habitual behavior. I hang on. I persist. You know the reductive, highly annoying maxim, "Don't get mad, get even"? Well, I get both angry *and* even. These were my steps to climb out of the deep hole—and I am not only talking about the money loss. Given how genetically impatient I am, there were three rather than twelve. I felt terrible, then mad, then determined. My partner Jeff used to joke that I am a race car with only two gears, first and fifth. I spent the better part of 2008 in first.

WANTED: WALL STREET

One interesting postscript to the crisis of 2008 is that taxpayers, who bailed out the banks, fared very well in the end. All federal rescue programs, most notably the Troubled Asset Relief Program (TARP), used to invest in financial institutions, and the loans to AIG turned out to be quite successful and profitable. The citizens were repaid with interest. There was no such intervention for hedge funds, I'm afraid. No taxpayer money was spent on hedge funds to shore them up or stabilize them. Of the roughly ten thousand in existence in 2008, about fifteen hundred closed. None was too big to fail, at least not at that time, unlike Long-Term Capital was deemed ten years before. The industry was decimated.

Feeling bad for the guy who loses his house is easy. It is harder to summon sympathy for the hedge fund manager who loses his investment job or his entire fund, but only after he has raked in heaps of dollars for over a decade. Even if the money lost came from government and corporate pension plans, university and museum endowments, and many other guardians of public money, there was no appetite for hedge fund bailouts. To the outside eye, all hedge funds were tainted by the same contemptible gob-smacking profits and rightfully deserved to fend for themselves. As a fund manager, I advise you to pick between billions and public sympathy because you're not going to get both. Did the average hedge fund manager consider himself liable for 2008, did he recalibrate his risk appetite? I don't know. We were not paid to be prudent. We were paid to take adequate risk for the reward it offered.

Hedge fund managers were thrown together with bankers, mortgage lenders, traders—anyone on Wall Street, really—into the vilification blender. I remember feeling an ambient disgust hanging around me like an unpleasant smell, and generally having thoughts like *I want to crawl into a hole*, or *I want to see my mom*.

My children had a monthly event called Bring Your Parent to School, when a self-respecting parent would visit the class to describe their job. There were physicians, professors, litigation lawyers even, and a smattering of entertainment folk. My son came back one day enthusiastically describing one classmate's father, a well-known movie producer who, according to my son, "wrote jokes and told actors what to do as his job." It all sounded very pleasant, if a little frivolous to me.

"Mama, will you come to school too?" my son asked.

"Of course, my bunny," I said. "As soon as you can guarantee me that I won't be lynched."

Anderson Cooper, the ever-noble CNN news anchor, came up with the engaging and rhythmically titled concept "Ten Most Wanted: Culprits of the Collapse." He introduced the nightly feature by saying, "This week and next week, every night, we will be adding a name to the list and telling you what they have done, and how much it's costing you. It's a rogues' gallery of Wall Street executives, politicians, and government officials who did not do their jobs. It's time you know their names, their faces. It's time they be asked to account for their actions."

I was in the habit of taking a long, relaxing bubble bath just around that hour, reflecting on the trading day and grimly pondering what the dickens I should do next. It was precisely then that my husband, a cold-blooded teaser with no regard to my fragile state of mind, always found it opportune to shout from the TV room, "Hey, you're still not in the top ten!"

CHAPTER 10

THE REBOUND BEGINS

It's easy to believe that you suck at your job after a tremendous failure, even when the carnage is everywhere. The right decision leading to 2008 was not to pick the best investments, it turns out; it was to buy nothing at all and hold cash or treasury bonds. One thing I learned out of this mess is that people are never as smart or as dumb as you think. (Except Rudy Giuliani; he really is as dumb as you think.)

In 2008, if a fund was long anything (meaning invested in—as opposed to being short or borrowing an asset to bet on its decline in price), it went down. If said fund held on and did nothing through 2009, it went back up. The market pendulum swung back in 2009 with full force. As much as 2008 was apocalyptically bad, with hedge funds as an asset class losing 19 percent, 2009 was epically good at positive 18.5 percent. All it took, really, was to stick around. There is the rub about macroeconomic forces: if the current is strong enough, it will overwhelm any manager's talent, wit, and skill.

Alas, many hedge funds did not have this luxurious option. Facing massive redemptions (the notice that investors give to get their money back—or what was left of it in 2008), they had to sell at the bottom of the market. In a perverse twist, hedge funds that held liquid assets such as stocks were forced to sell because they could. Others, distressed funds in particular, were confronted with such an illiquid market that they quite simply could neither sell assets nor honor redemptions, at least not in full. So they simply closed their redemption windows, just like a bank at the end of a working day. Many put up what the industry called "redemption gates," which froze investors' money until a future date or compelled them to spread their redemptions over several quarters. Some segregated their assets into tradeable and non-tradeable pools. Redemptions could come only from the tradeable pool.

The flip side is that precluding some investors from redeeming their investments turned out to be a great favor, a lucky break for most of them. It was the best way, indeed the only way, to make the money back. If you were down deep double digits in 2008 and quit the game, you were out. The end. If you subsequently decided to put your money back in 2009, you bought higher *and* you were charged fees all over again, for it was logically considered a brand-new investment. If you had instead, say, hibernated for eighteen months or taken a leisurely trip to Mars, you returned to gasp in horror at a loss of 19 percent in 2008 only to guffaw at a profit of 19 percent in 2009 and marvel that no hedge fund fees were due until your first dollar was recouped. It made for a year and a half of investment management for free.

THE SAME, BUT DIFFERENT

The Global Financial Crisis had been a liquidity crisis; liquidity was now aggressively pumped back into the system. Throughout the fall of 2008, the Federal Reserve introduced programs to facilitate further lending to an ever-increasing list of financial institutions who would accept an ever-increasing list of additional types of collateral. It got so ridiculous that I planned on showing up at the Fed window for a personal loan with a rusty tricycle as a guarantee of repayment. The government invested preferred equity in eight of the biggest U.S. banks to strengthen their capital structure and ensure their viability: Bank of America/Merrill Lynch, Bank of New York Mellon, Citigroup, Goldman Sachs, J.P. Morgan, Morgan Stanley, State Street, and Wells Fargo. Not only were financial institutions shored up and rescued, so were auto manufacturers GM and Chrysler, mortgage providers Fannie Mae and Freddie Mac, and insurance giant AIG.

Money started to circulate again and gradually, investors, banks, pensions, mutual funds, and hedge funds regained the ability to invest and transact. The government had orchestrated a massive intervention to restore the flow of money and, just as importantly, confidence in the system. It worked. After the most dramatic plunge in 2008, markets around the world rebounded energetically in 2009. The crisis was much like childbirth, excruciatingly painful but shockingly brief, relatively speaking. Ignoring that hedge funds lost more money in 2008 than they made in the previous ten years, investors—who either forgot or forgave—came back, and brought more of their friends with them.

However, when hedge fund investors returned, it was not quite business as usual. They now had a different mindset—one where they had grown wary of smaller funds. The belief now was that with size came safety. For a smallish, single open-ended fund (meaning investors can invest when they please and redeem every quarter), losing half its assets means a drop in fees so dramatic that it cannot sustain the fixed cost structure anymore and leads almost inevitably to the firm's closure. Research shows that even in a good economy, nearly half of hedge funds never reach their fifth year of existence. Prior to 2008, being small had been an advantage. Early investors had turned to hedge funds to produce outsized profits by being quick and flexible, exploiting market inefficiencies produced by large market players weighed down by inertia and size.

The Global Financial Crisis changed everything. Investors realized that hedge funds were not, by and large, hedged. Barring a few exceptions, they tanked with the market. A positively inclined spin doctor would highlight that hedge funds were down only 19 percent in 2008, while the S&P 500 was down 37 percent. The truth is that hedge funds were not supposed to produce superior *relative* returns; the goal was to produce *persistent absolute positive* returns. To be hedged means to deliver profit regardless of the direction of the market, as was the case during the telecom crisis. Hedge funds did not deliver on that promise in 2008. Every hedge fund category but one (managed futures, a subset so nebulous that I really have no clue what they do) produced a negative return.

CHANGING THE MODEL

2008 did not just shake investors, it also provided a wake-up call to hedge fund managers. They realized how fragile and unstable the existing business model was. The crisis served as a catalyst for the entire industry to seek scale and diversification rather than reside within specialization and nimbleness. A changing investor base was willing to sacrifice returns for safety. We happily obliged. Structural variations were launched, including locked-up funds, delayed draws, and return hurdles. New products were added, such as collateralized loan obligations, direct lending, long-only low-fee vehicles, and industry-specific or asset-specific pools. The name of the game became to offer a one-stop shopping experience, by which I mean the ability to sell and cross-sell worldwide, from the Hong Kong Monetary Authority to a billionaire's family office and the New York State pension plan. No matter your investment preference, time horizon, or risk appetite, we have a fund for you! To stay in existence, hedge funds looked to expand, attract "sticky money" (hedge fund slang for investors that will stay around for the long term), and accrue franchise value. The bigger they got, the bigger they became, like a snowball rolling down a mountain.

Hedge fund traders had matured into empire builders.

Canyon was no different and the few years after 2008 saw the launch of a structured product fund and a locked-up distressed vehicle. We had lost assets during the Global Financial Crisis but were working our size back up to $20 billion. The employee count was increasing. Hedge funds that were already big ships were on their way to becoming supertankers. But this growth explosion had grave consequences for liquidity and flexibility. The two original sources of hedge fund competitive "edges" mostly went out the window.

The Efficient Market Hypothesis, a cornerstone of modern finance usually associated with a paper by Eugene Fama and Paul Samuelson in 1970, proposes that asset prices fully reflect available information and that, as a result, consistently beating the market is impossible. An important assumption here is that liquidity is perfect, that there always are willing buyers and sellers. As far as I can tell from my twenty years of investing, there are fatal flaws in the application of the theory into practice. Academics usually dispute the information piece, but I'd like to highlight the problem associated with the notion of perfect liquidity.

Supply and demand are rarely in equilibrium in a market. If a holder wants to sell an outsize block of bonds or stocks in a tight time frame, he might not find a buyer at the efficient price and be forced instead to sell at a discount. The reverse is true for a large buyer, who might have to pay a premium for size. This goes for any asset. If your company relocates you to a different office and gives you a month to move your family and sell your house, you are likely looking at a rotten, inefficient deal, particularly if yours is the largest property on the block. What happens when hedge funds themselves grow so big that they become the source, and therefore the victims, of illiquidity and inertia? Fat funds cannot beat the market, they *are* the market. In the first decade of the industry, it was not rare to see forced sellers, such as a mutual fund whose mandate prohibits holding bonds of a bankrupt or downgraded company, or an insurance company that faces a large claim and needs cash. These types of investors sometimes have to cope with investment constraints beyond pure trading-profit maximization. Hedge funds, on the other hand, were the rare breed that could buy when others had to sell and sell when others had to buy. They were the buyers or sellers of last resort and in such capacity, generally if not consistently, commanded a better execution price. If there is a forced seller and few viable buyers, the buyer gets a good deal. But if ten thousand (the approximate current count) hedge fund buyers line up to compete for the trade, then by definition it is not a forced sale anymore. Not to mention that by 2009, most traditional investors had wised up and learned to hold on and not press the panic-sell button.

BUFFETT'S BET

In a nutshell, alpha generation disappeared. Simplistically put, alpha is the part of the return that is uncorrelated to the overall performance of the market, while beta is the bit that depends on the direction of the market. I am not suggesting, of course, that some hedge funds did not beat the market sometimes—what I am saying is that *persistent, absolute* outperformance ended around 2009. That year, hedge funds were up almost 19 percent and distressed hedge funds almost 21 percent, yet they underperformed most indices. The S&P was up over 26 percent, high-yield bonds over 58 percent, and emerging markets over 78 percent. It was the first time after five consecutive years of outperformance that hedge funds lagged the S&P. It would be followed by many, many more. Between 2009 and 2017, neither hedge funds in general nor distressed funds in particular beat the S&P 500 in a *single* year.

The Oracle of Omaha saw this coming, but perhaps not for the reason that everyone thinks. There was another mounting problem for hedge funds. In 2007, Warren Buffett bet $1 million that investment professionals could not put together a portfolio of hedge funds that would outperform an S&P 500 index fund over a ten-year period. The bet ended in December 31, 2017, and you guessed it, Buffett won.

On that exact day, I quit in a regal display of integrity and intestinal fortitude.

I'm kidding. It was pure coincidence.

During the ten-year period of Buffett's bet, the S&P index fund returned 7.1 percent compounded annually versus the 2.2 percent average return of a basket of five hedge funds handpicked by Ted Seides, then an asset manager with Protégé Partners, the only fund that stepped forward to pick up the gauntlet.

Why did Buffett issue the challenge? Certainly not because he could predict the stock market. It was purely and simply a question of fees. He explained it thusly in a 2016 shareholder letter: "In Berkshire Hathaway's 2005 annual report, I argued that active investment management by professionals—in aggregate—would over a period of years underperform the returns achieved by rank amateurs who simply sat still. I explained that the massive fees levied by a variety of "helpers" would leave their clients—again in aggregate—worse off than if the amateurs simply invested in an unmanaged low-cost index fund."

It wasn't a judgment of the ability of any particular hedge fund manager. It was a bet that the industry had matured and was now charging so much that net returns, that is to say after paying fees, would not beat the market anymore. The outperformance ship had sailed.

The industry changes were so profound, the abyss of 2008 was so searing, and the 2009 rebound so befuddling that they forced me to broaden my perspective. I took a step back. Rather than evaluating my portfolio, my performance, and my firm, I tried for the first time to reflect on the roots of the crisis and the structural flaws of the hedge fund industry. The succeeding year, around 2010, was a period of private turmoil. The concept of survival rose to the top of my mind when my mother was diagnosed with cancer. I was far away and unable to help her or my father much, practically or morally. I started questioning some of my choices—including living abroad and having little free time. To a French person, two weeks of vacation in the summer is little more than foreplay.

Personal matters and private development took precedent over professional growth and brought lasting changes to my life.

PERSONAL ENDEAVORS

I forever felt that there was a chasm between those who had gone through 2008–2009, the survivors, the veterans, and those who had not. The Global Crisis was like a near-death experience. Psychologists report that those who come in contact with the other side can subsequently show a profound change in their attitude in the aftermath. They tend to be more open, caring, and loving. I can honestly witness that I became none of that. But here is something I can subscribe to: there is allegedly a new awareness of meaning and purpose in experiencers' lives. If by "meaning" and "purpose," one means putting more energy and time into fun, exciting, non-professional activities, then that was definitely my case.

Going to a museum is therapeutic and healing to me, an infallible tool when I find myself muddled, which was my state of mind for the better part of 2008 to 2010. Seeing familiar paintings and recognizing the artists feels like meeting close friends. They comfort me, except they don't speak and I don't talk back. That is way beyond what I can ask from even my BFF.

I bought art with my very first paycheck in 1992, a set of Japanese woodblock prints by Kunisada. These were quite affordable at the time and particularly dear to me because they were a tremendous source of inspiration to the post-Impressionist painters, such as Pierre Bonnard, Paul Sérusier, and Édouard Vuillard, whom I had adored since I was a girl. Those artists were quite unaffordable to me back then, but their inspiration was not. By 2009, however, I had enough income to acquire works by the painters themselves (not to mention that the art market was in as much a disarray as the financial markets) and start collecting in earnest. I could hang my friends on the wall. Said like that it sounds weird, but the joy these pictures give me is boundless and everlasting.

Collecting progressively evolved into a social activity as well, opening my life up to people in the art world, who, if I am honest here, mostly value my husband's company and knowledge. We met and befriended curators, auctioneers, collectors, conservators, historians—all folks from a radically different walk of life and with whom we shared a passion. By the way, in my arbitrary and supercilious value system, while it is *not* OK to spend millions on a car, it is understandable, nay, even commendable for a work of art—except one by Jeff Koons. Naturally, we do a lot of research to figure out if the price of a painting is fair, but I never buy anything as an investment. In fact, it saps my spirit when I meet collectors (and there are quite a few among my esteemed hedge fund peers) who prate on about what a great deal they got on an art piece. It's a suitable answer when asked about a family-sized pack of double-roll toilet paper from Costco—less so for a Matisse. Call me fastidious, but I find it more stimulating to talk about why it speaks to you, how it fits with the other paintings in a collection, why the period interests you, what the story behind its creation is, or how you felt when you first saw the piece. I can never remember offhand how much things cost. But I know precisely why I own a picture.

Around the same time, I started playing polo (on a horse, not in the water). I appreciate this sounds like a clear-cut diagnosis of middle-age crisis. It's completely true—but let me explain the context anyway. My husband and I had planned a summer vacation to Mongolia, complete with a four-day horseback riding trek. About a week prior to the trip, we discovered that the fine print, which had inexplicably escaped us thus far, specified, "Riding experience recommended." I had never been on a horse. He had been thrown off one once upon a time. So off we went to take riding lessons near our house in Los Angeles. Then we embarked on a truly memorable trip, and not just because I suffered from a pernicious stomach bug that had me come out of the tent in the frigid night half a dozen times. It is singularly cold and lonely to spill your guts in the steppe of Mongolia in the wee hours. Every morning, our tall and handsome horseman, fittingly named Hoiga—I actually have no idea whether it means anything, but it sounds manly—wrapped my waist with a wide and stiff band of fabric so tightly that I could hardly breathe or move, propped me upright on the horse, gave it a good smack, and instructed me to gallop close to him for four hours. Exquisite agony.

Naturally, I stuck with riding after the trip. It's not just that I am a sucker for physical punishment with a particular liking for dangerous activities like backcountry skiing (which I practice in the winter), skydiving (which I tried with my father), and bungee jumping (which I tried from a hot-air balloon). I simply love learning—almost anything. As an adult, I have taken classes in ballet, surfing, boxing, and recently tai chi, not to mention art history, Tibetan Buddhism, Japanese, and floor tiling. I am not particularly good at anything. I just enjoy the journey.

My riding lessons took place in the outdoor arena of a state park in California. It happened to be right above the last remaining polo field in Los Angeles, and my husband offered a solution to my growing boredom with figure-eight and horse-grooming exercises.

"Why don't you try *that?*" he said, pointing to a polo game one day. "How hard can it be?"

My first lessons were a far cry from the glamorous image that polo may have. It took place in the evening, in an equestrian facility that had seen better days, deep into the Santa Monica Canyon. Every inch in the tack room was covered by years of spiderwebs and layers of dust; you could hide a dead body in there with absolute impunity. The instructor, a chain-smoking middle-age woman with infinite patience, a deep-throated voice, and a golden heart, charged seventy dollars for the lesson, including the horse. This so-called sport of kings/king of sports cost less than an hour of personal training.

I bought my first horse in December 2009 and played my first chukker on grass in 2011. So began an enduring passion and life-long pursuit. They say that polo is more addictive and more dangerous than cocaine. I got hooked quickly and incurably. My life became a journey marked by the exhilarating and frustrating pursuit, on the back of very noble animals, of a hard little ball that once landed full force in my face and broke my nose and right cheekbone. I love it.

The polo world has similarities to that of the hedge funds. There are quite a few women at the entry and middle levels, but it's male-dominated at the top. The playing field, like a trading floor, is usually dense with testosterone and echoes of choice words, although voiced in various languages. Everyone is super competitive; everyone wants to win. From my amateur observation, the scale and financial means of a polo outfit, like a hedge fund, can rig the game or heavily tip it in its favor. Like the hedge fund professionals, the polo pros make money while customers (called patrons) pay to play. Similarly, pros constantly pitch their services and skills to the next client. They keep cool in the middle of chaos. But there are differences too. Polo pros put their lives on the line; they possess extraordinary physical strength, balance, coordination, and horsemanship skills. Hedge fund managers generally do not. And of course, none of the former are billionaires and none of the latter are hot. In polo, I not only met an entirely new community but found two figures who were profoundly missing from my professional life. The first is the woman who takes care of my horses, the barn, the games, and the logistics and has steadfastly advised, encouraged, and pushed me to become a better rider, player, and horse owner. Hurtling on a thousand-pound animal at thirty miles an hour with seven other players vying for a ball the size of a tennis ball but as hard as a golf ball can put your life at risk. She is as close to a female partner as I will ever have. And the second is a high-level patron who, for no obvious reason other than to help me advance in the sport, recurrently invited me to play on his team at a competitive level, showing no frustration at my mistakes and shortcomings but patiently explaining the right moves, the better play, the winning strategy, and the long game. He is the mentor I never had on Wall Street.

I have long since my beginning days replaced the initial instructor with Argentinean pros—who are considerably more expensive but nicer to look at. They all have the same advice: "Keep your head down, Dominique."

In polo as in everything else, I suppose.

I have diplomas in Dragon
Management and Virgin Reclamation.
My horse is the latest model, with
Automatic transmission and built-in
Obsolescence. My spear is custom-built,
And my prototype armour
Still on the secret list. You can't
Do better than me at the moment.

—U. A. FANTHORPE,
"Not My Best Side"

CHAPTER 11

ROOM AT THE TOP

In 2012, the two founding partners of Canyon made the strategic decision to elevate a select few to partnership status. This was not only a prestigious title and the highest level of seniority at the firm, it also meant a different compensation scheme. In the industry, partners generally earn a percentage of the incentive fees of the firm and, should the firm be sold, get a cut on the upside. Partners feel more like owners than employees. This new partnership structure did not emerge just out of a generous desire to share the wealth, although I could conceive that it was a large contributor to it—if I were an ingénue rather than a trader, that is. No, it was chiefly a thoughtful retention plan, spurred, I reckon, by the unexpected departure of Canyon's most senior employee and head of research. Turnover is harmful to any business, but it is particularly damaging to hedge funds, who have no other assets than the brain-power and expertise of their employees.

I made the cut. I was the only female of the additional seven partners in Canyon's initial expansion, and the sole female portfolio manager. I was used to this, of course. In most meetings, both in-house and on the road, there was usually one woman—yours truly—as compared to eight or more men. My recurring joke before sitting down to a business dinner was, "Shall we do one girl, one boy around the table?" I know, it's not particularly funny. But then again, neither are wisecracks about women's purses (messy, expensive, and proliferating) and women's shoes (uncomfortable, expensive, and proliferating). If I may offer an unbidden word of wisdom to all funnymen out there on Wall Street, these jokes are, at best, tedious.

Understand one thing: there were, and still are, doggedly few senior women in hedge funds and almost none in the position of investing. You will find women in investment banks (corporate finance, capital markets, and sales and trading), including some in senior positions. Corporate law firms are likewise relatively diverse in gender. But as far as women in hedge funds, zilch. According to a 2015 survey by EY, KPMG, and Morningstar, only 2 percent of hedge funds are run by women. Less than one in twenty hedge funds employs a female portfolio manager. Female-run funds manage less than 1 percent of the industry assets. And so it goes with the depressing numbers, but you get the picture. And why is that, pray? Because change requires impetus and incentives. Unless clients require hedge funds to have women on their teams and refuse to invest in funds that do not, there is no external incentive. BlackRock, State Street, and Fidelity paved the way in 2017, when they tackled the issue of diversity on the boards of public companies. They pressured companies and threatened to vote against sitting directors at companies with boards made up only of men. It worked. Women now hold 28 percent of all board seats at major corporations. Only one S&P 500 company is left with an all-male board. After a California law required that all public companies based in the state have at least one woman director by the end of last year and three by the end of 2021, women claimed almost half of new board seats.

And until hedge funds have internalized data that demonstrates heterogeneous investment teams outperform homogeneous ones, there is no impetus either. Abundant research from both the private sector and academia proves the efficacy of diversity in corporate profit, growth, and decision-making—trust me, it applies to hedge funds too. Imagine my annoyance reading this quote in a *Business Insider* article from a headhunter at Long Ridge Partners, a specialized recruiting firm for the investment management industry: "Most funds want to go out and hire the best talent. They don't care if it's a man or a woman." Alas, it is hard to so thoroughly miss the point. Does he ever watch sports? It isn't the best talent that wins; it's the best team. A great baseball team doesn't have nine great hitters. Even I know that, and no one ever called me a sports fan.

Absent both incentives and impetus, no amount of Sheryl Sandberg's call to "lean in" will make a difference to *average* numbers. At the margin, will it help *some* women forge a trailblazing path? Absolutely. Just as I hope that my own technique will. In keeping with a two-word commandment, I opt to hang on. Or I raise you to three: stick with it. As for societal changes, however, a motto will not do. To lean in, you must first be let in.

In distressed investing, it's even rarer to find women at the top. Anecdotally (although it in fact may turn out to be statistically significant), in my twenty years of working for a hedge fund, I have met *one* other female partner, Meridee Moore.

Meridee was a pioneer in distressed investing. After ten years working for the hedge fund of Tom Steyer (yes, as in the 2020 democratic presidential candidate) in the '90s and becoming the only female partner, she hung out her shingle in 2002. Watershed Asset Management managed over $2 billion in assets in the heyday and became an extraordinarily successful fund. Here is where it gets interesting, though. She decided to shut down in 2015 and proceeded to return all external capital. Not because she had lost money—*au contraire*—or had reached an age at which you would hesitate to give anyone your kid's monthly allowance anyway (Carl Icahn is eighty-four years old—think about that). No, she believed that the field was too crowded, the alpha generators gone, and future returns not high enough for the fees. She turned out to be prescient and a pioneer there too. We had a working relationship for over two decades until we served together as independent directors on a corporate board. We became friends despite her incessant use of the most obscure and perplexing—at least to a non-native speaker—American colloquialisms. She had me mesmerized the first time she admonished us directors to "keep our knees bent." It turned out to simply mean to be ready—did everyone else know that?—but I quietly resolved to enhance both my vocabulary and my investing acumen through the relationship.

Meridee exhibited all the right pedigrees. She was a lawyer by trade but had worked for Lehman Brothers. She had coauthored a chapter on distressed bank debt trading with Marty Whitman for the economist, professor, and prolific author Frank Fabozzi (whose books you no doubt own, if you've ever taken a finance class). She joined the hedge fund world at the right time and traded some incredibly complex situations, including the liquidations of investment firm Drexel Burnham Lambert and Integrated Resources, when distressed trading was in its infancy. She was the only female investor and made partner within a year at Farallon

Capital Management. Being a woman was an "advantage," she said, because CEOs remembered her and lawyers and traders liked her. Raising money in 2002 to open Watershed, her own fund, was relatively "easy"; she had great references and a ten-year track record of making money. Most important, she had the Farallon brand recognition and a large seed investment from Tom Steyer. I had to dig hard to hear even a smidge of frustration with the male environment she had worked in all her life. "I just put my head down and competed," she explained. When I finally extracted them from her, some of her experiences echoed mine, including the internal scuffles and battle to retain her best analysts. One was different and revealing. Investors had expected her to perform better—i.e., lose less money—in the Global Financial Crisis of 2008 than her male counterparts. "Because I am a woman," she told me, "I think investors assumed me to be more risk averse." Of course, said investors would have surely taken their money out if she had indeed been more risk averse and produced less profit *before* the crash. Further, Meridee confirmed my view that after the crisis, money allocators started favoring large funds over return potential. "The ex-Goldman Sachs guys running sizeable institutions became an easier choice."

"Because of safer returns?" I asked.

"Safer, yes, but not in terms of returns," she responded, "safer for the allocators' jobs. No one in their investment committees would question the decision to go with a known quantity. A lot of them were scared and perceived sticking with a mid-size fund run by a woman as an added risk."

Watershed's performance in the top third of funds allowed it to survive the crisis and retain over $1 billion of assets. It illustrated stunningly well the research papers that find that, although the performance of female hedge fund managers is equal or better, they consistently attract fewer assets.[9] Women must *outperform* men if they want to stay in the business, but even when they do, investors are reluctant to entrust them with their money, thereby keeping women's funds small. After 2008, size itself became a detractor. The vicious loop was closed.

If I assembled all the female senior investors I know in hedge funds, we would hardly constitute a book club. Mind you, I would boldly suggest that we all read my book, which would provide me with a small but passionate reader base.

Five years after I became a partner, the *Hedge Fund Journal* selected me for their annual ranking of the Top 50 Women in Hedge Funds. To get to the number fifty, a large swath of those women included were not in hedge funds at all but rather bankers, accountants, and lawyers. Of the hedge fund women per se, a minority of us were investors, while a majority worked in the "soft" departments like marketing and investor relations. These are not the profit centers, and their members are not the big moneymakers. I was immodestly pleased with this inclusion, as you can imagine, and my husband ceremoniously announced its publication to our children over dinner. One of them ruminated on the startling fact that there really were, what, as many as fifty women in my business? The other one raised an eyebrow and inquired suspiciously, "Exactly *which* number are you?"

A young woman named Lauren Bonner was interviewed by the *New Yorker* because she sued the prominent hedge fund Point72 (started by Steve Cohen, the one who supposedly inspired the TV show *Billions*) for sexual discrimination. Her case, filed in the Southern District Court of New York, is a worthwhile read. There is the whiteboard with the word "PUSSY" hanging in the president's office—yes, all caps; why be subtle? There is the episode at a fundraiser where a business associate, when asked about the name of his female guest by a male portfolio manager standing by Lauren, responded, "Why? Do you want to fuck her? You can.

She works for me." In addition to the investment meetings that the COO preemptively qualified as "no girls allowed," the sexist numbers—in hires, promotions, and pay scale—revealed a horror show of a company. Of course, this is the plaintiff's side, but it is hard not to form a point of view of the sort of place that Point72 was. The suit was eventually brought to arbitration, as mandated by her employment agreement, and settled in September 2020.

However, what interested me most is what Lauren Bonner so judiciously said in a March 2018 interview about working at a hedge fund. "It's a small club and it's an all-boys club, and people are terrified of not getting another job. Women start to develop a sense of…'God, I'm lucky to even be here.'"

I find her brave for publicly saying so. It was certainly true for me. On the other hand, I *was* lucky, lucky enough not to be bogged down by the type of behavior she had to endure. I will venture to say that all women who make it in the finance field have stomached some form of institutionalized or blatant discrimination. But I do believe there are two types: passive sexism and active sexism. Passive sexism consists of preconceived ideas about women, clichés, societal expectations, antiquated behaviors, and harebrained judgments. All women on Wall Street have experienced it their entire career. It's always in the air, like the pungent smell of testosterone. It runs the gamut from unthinkingly incidental, as heard when someone starts a meeting with "Hello, gentlemen," to a trifle offensive, as seen each time a trader asked my junior analysts, "What does Dominique look like?" My answer to someone who wondered about my physique was, "Is the bond cheaper if I'm good-looking?"

Passive sexism is surmountable with resilience and humor. Active sexism, actual discrimination or harassment, is not.

I was lucky at Canyon and Lauren was unlucky at Point72. At Canyon, I had partners who were respectful. It does not follow that there was no "ambient" sexism—a passing comment, a dopey joke, an unwelcome look. But Canyon employees followed the founding partners' lead—they had to—and these two men entrusted me with the highest level of seniority. They were very public and unabashed about it. I was once given a preprinted name tag at a conference that read "Dominique Mielle, Canyon Capital, Analyst." I made a mild effort to find the twit who had confused me with a lowly junior person, then gamely put it on anyway, head high. When I stopped by to chat with one of the partners during the day, he immediately spotted the label on my jacket. Before I could say ineptitude, he yanked it off, reached for a pen, crossed off the erroneous title and wrote in large capital letters *PARTNER*.

"Much better," he said, but I was not entirely sure about that. Who is so petty, so staunchly attached to a fancy title as to walk around with a hand-redrawn name tag? I was, apparently.

ALL ABOUT CLOs

Becoming a partner fueled my ambition and allowed it to take off. By 2012, that ambition had me seeking ownership and leadership. I wanted to run my own show. After the 2008 dramatic crash and the 2009 smashing rebound, it became clear that hedge funds needed to diversify. They required greater scale, stickier money, and more product lines in order to become real enterprises and build franchise value. Out of this realization came a few ideas, including collateralized loan obligations, or CLOs. These were not new. CLOs had existed for over a decade, with some structural advances over the years and a long issuance hiatus during the Global Financial Crisis. What was novel was the trend of hedge funds systematically expanding their business expertise into new types of investment vehicles. Canyon was no longer strictly and simplistically a "hedge fund"; it became an "alternative investment manager." And so it went for all our large competitors.

At the risk of putting you into a deep slumber, I shall endeavor to describe what a CLO is. In a CLO structure, managers raise money by issuing tranches of bonds and equity to outside investors all over the world. The collected capital is used to buy loans (about two to three hundred loans, each $2 million to $5 million in size) issued by a variety of corporations that everyone will be familiar with (from Pizza Hut to Dell Computers to Waste Management). Payments coming into the CLO from the bundle of loans first pay interest and principal on the CLO bonds. What is left goes to the equity holders. The goal is to produce enough payments from the pool of loans to produce the greatest possible residual to send to the equity while safely ensuring that the CLO bonds are paid on a timely basis. For his valiant effort, said CLO manager collects a small annual fee (generally 0.5 percent of the assets) plus an incentive fee. Although these fees are infinitely less remunerative than the hedge fund fees, they are much more stable, as they run over the life of the CLO, which is typically five to seven years.

We only had issued and managed a handful of CLOs in the previous decade. It was an ad hoc business. We had not thought of systematically developing it or building a team to grow it, market it, and consider it one of multiple offerings to sell to investors. In September 2012, at the end of the annual research retreat, which had taken place in a waterfront park in Malibu, the freshly elected partners sat in the community room for a strategy session. The founding partners went around the team assigning new potential investment projects. They offered me two. I rejected one but enthusiastically accepted to spearhead CLOs.

I believed in the product, and rightly so, if I may say so myself. In 2012, Canyon was not a recognized CLO manager, nor did we have any clout in the area with either investors or brokers. I turned a rather moribund and sorry affair into a $3.5 billion dollar business in five years. Where we had done exactly zero CLO deals in the previous six years, we issued eight in the six years after I took over, and they all thrived.

About five thousand CLOs have been issued over the past thirty years, and Moody's, Standard & Poor's, and Fitch, who rate the bond tranches, have tracked most of them. A handful of specialized research analysts within investment banks also record data, analyze them, and publish reports. It is a statistically and historically rich field. At the outset of my work, I pored over the performance and behavior of CLOs over the years, paying particularly close attention to the 2006–2007 vintage deals that went through the 2008 crisis. There is no sense in denying it, I fancy data manipulation. I have a real fondness for financial modeling and scenario analyses. I am an enthusiast for statistical simulations.

Imagine you bought loans of companies that subsequently, foolishly, go bankrupt. What happens next? Worse, say the entire market tanks and, sinking with it, all the loans the CLO holds. How low is the correlation between the stock and loan market, and does it hold in times of crashes? Imagine, pray, that interest rates go out of kilter. Or suppose that the default rate, prepayment, or recovery rates run amok. What's up with your CLO then? All these assumptions and many more can be tested, twisted, engineered, reverse engineered, and all the results shown to answer potential investors' questions.

NOT BAD. GOOD!

By that point in my career, four analysts were reporting to me in my capacity as hedge fund portfolio manager. I was one of five senior portfolio managers, directing the investment of some $20 billion in hedge fund assets. The CLO was distinct and separate, though.

For one thing, it was an entire business rather than just a portfolio of investments, and leading a business was a new job. I managed everything from marketing to structuring to staffing to investing. I added three people under my direct supervision, including Jeff, a top-notch marketer and structurer (who had been at Canyon for a decade) and who became one of my best friends to boot. I deepened my relationships with our internal investor relations and marketing department. There is investing and then there is the business of investing. The latter is not only about picking bonds and loans. It involves strategy and people. What am I selling? How am I to sell it? What is my competitive edge? Who are my investors? What is my go-to-market plan?

I set goals in terms of billions under management within three years—which the partners promptly asked me to multiply by three (the assets, not the time frame) since they regarded me as the head of the project. But building Canyon's reputation in the CLO business took time, and the first meetings were quite simply appalling. Perhaps the most emblematic one came on my first trip to Japan, circa 2012, with my team of three. The room was stiflingly hot and noisy as hell, with relentless loud banging above our heads. It is always muggy in Japanese offices in the summer, even for a non-American, but the construction hullabaloo was novel. Our potential Japanese investors plus the interpreter filed in, took their seats, and within minutes fell asleep. Not dozing off, you understand, not snoozing with the occasional lifting of an eyelid, pretending to care. I mean a deep, drooling-at-the-mouth sort of stupor. And this was all six of them. It was as if they had come to my meeting *to* sleep.

I went through my presentation, as rehearsed, for a dense forty-five minutes, modulated my voice, reformulated sentences into questions in the hope that someone would budge, took off my jacket, then put it back on to create some air traffic. No sign of life. I thought of Khrushchev with sympathy and experienced more than a fleeting urge to bang my shoe on the table (no, on their heads. With the heel). No one did anything to prevent me from reaching the inevitable conclusion of my speech until at last one of them woke up and talked to the interpreter, who translated thusly: "We like to invest with investors who are good and Canyon is bad. Why do you want us to invest with a bad manager?"

The question was factually phrased but so fundamentally and alarmingly wrong. I was mute for a thick minute. It was all so spirit-sapping.

"We are not bad," I said with a forced smile that reeked of resignation. "We are good. I'll go through the numbers again."

As you may have surmised, we did not get a single Japanese investor that time. It took another two years of meetings more or less like that one or worse to get them through the door.

Our main investor ended up being JP Morgan. I met the head of the treasury department, who happened to be a Stanford Business School alumnus and had graduated a year before I had. The entire team was present in a formal boardroom so vast that I was convinced it would echo my wild and noisy heartbeats. He was clearly in charge—a potential ally, maybe not positively inclined but at least open-minded. This was not a drill. It was showtime. We had a fruitful meeting, but he remained skeptical when I asked for a response a few days later. Why should he invest with a new manager? He had dozens to choose from already, known quantities and qualified. Being a new manager was many steps above being called a bad one as far as I was concerned. I was genuinely exhilarated.

"Look," I said—or implored, rather—"I need you to show up and invest in my deal. Period. What is it going to take? I will get you such a good deal that your board will kiss your feet. I am going to produce returns that will make you beg for the next deal." Well, I did not use those exact terms, but you get my drift.

So he gamely named his price, and let me take this opportunity to thank and salute him. It was a blood-sucking deal and left virtually no room to pay our management fees, but I hardly had a choice. He was my only prospect. Therefore, I did the logical thing. I shook hands and set out to find another spot in the transaction to squeeze money out of. Our own broker, Morgan Stanley, who was helping us sell the deal, saw a sudden and rather unpleasant cut in *their* fees.

This was the first but not the last piece of the complicated structure that is a CLO. Putting all the pieces together to go ahead and issue a CLO is a delicate balance, an exquisitely complicated puzzle. I needed bond investors beyond the JP Morgan lead, I needed equity investors, and I had to start buying loans to populate my asset pool. You need outside money to purchase loans, but you need an initial pool of loans to convince outside investors that you know how to invest in a solid portfolio. If the market goes up in price, you can show a nice gain in the loans you have already bought, but it's harder to buy the next ones. If the market goes down, new loans are more attractively priced, but your existing portfolio shows a loss—which is appalling to potential investors. Anything can happen. Anything can go wrong at any point.

The founding partners were only loosely involved in the structuring and marketing aspects. For the most part, their opinion was that, what with this being a Canyon product and all, and Canyon being one of the largest, most reputable fixed income managers around, investors were surely tripping all over each other to put money in. How could we *not* get investors?

The truth is that we were indeed well established in many areas, just not this one. This was our first CLO in years (six to be exact). Investors were most definitely not going to airily take a chance on us.

The first deal was a huge challenge. Then, once over that hurdle, it had to become a volume business because the fees were so small. As soon as I got one under my belt, I was already thinking about lining up investors for the next vehicle. I had to get on the road every six months and, incidentally, find a new broker since Morgan Stanley was slightly miffed at my unceremonious sacrifice of their hard-earned fees. CLOs, in this respect, fit very well with the hedge fund business in general. There is a five-minute celebration over one trade and then you are on to the next.

It suited me just fine. My husband has often remarked that the job was perfect for me because I can hardly stand still long enough to enjoy the moment after an accomplishment. Honestly, I completely can. Just not for *very* long. He claims that I perpetually need to be entertained. "It's a profession," he once said, "to constantly delight you." I could tell he meant it was his. I do hate downtime. In French, it is called "dead time."

DIALING FOR DOLLARS

My success in growing the CLO business, then later in raising a CLO-dedicated equity fund, a complicated, first-of-its-kind product, led to exponentially greater visibility—to investors, but also internally. The marketing group noticed I could sell and that I genuinely enjoyed it. They then started using a lot more of me to market the hedge fund as well.

It was an interesting, if late, realization in my career that I am a rather capable salesperson. Theretofore, I intervened now and again to talk to investors when the marketing people or the founding partners asked me to. When I started treating CLOs as my own cottage industry, I realized that the biggest challenge of the business was to secure investors, which required an investment strategy, a marketing plan, a selling presentation, a well-rehearsed pitch, and a litany of other tools. But mostly it required building personal relationships. There may be dozens of phone calls and hundreds of emails before a physical presentation. Still, meeting in person is critical—no, indispensable—to generate the level of interest and trust required for investors to commit hundreds of millions of dollars.

So on the road I went.

CHAPTER 12

ON THE ROAD

To build the CLO business, I traveled to Europe, Japan, Korea, China, Hong Kong, Singapore, and all over the U.S. I don't mean to spit in the soup, as we say in French; it is a luxurious way to get around. You stay in five-star hotels, fly business class, and eat in Michelin restaurants. You are driven around in black Mercedes by affable men who carry your luggage, open the car door, and ask if the air-conditioning temperature is to your liking. While I did travel extensively with my parents as a child, and then on my own as a student, it was on a considerably tighter budget. My parents, who in fairness traveled quite comfortably for their generation of cheapskates, had a few sanctified rules. One was "Thou shall consume nothing from the minibar." "Thou shall not order room service" was another command, which, frankly, I have come to embrace because the food takes forever, usually arrives cold and is beginning to congeal, and, let's face it, it is rather sad to eat dinner alone in front of a TV and in your bathrobe. My children, on the other hand, do not abide by any of these rules. The minibar is breakfast, room service is dinner, and business class is in their travel policy for flights over ten hours. I am lucky that they do not touch the mini liquor bottles…yet. Don't get me wrong, I know how bratty it sounds. But I will not apologize for being financially successful, nor should anyone whose wealth was acquired through hard work, well-timed bravery and…luck.

All of this notwithstanding, you would be wrong to assume that roadshow trips were the height of glamour. The plush velvety robe usually stayed untouched, the spa and swimming pool unvisited. I was lucky if I could hit the gym and the bar at least once—preferably in that order. We flew a ridiculous number of miles. We ate at the finest restaurants, if your definition of eating is in fact going over twenty PowerPoint slides, answering questions thoughtfully, selling yourself diplomatically, and swallowing the duck magret all at once and inside of the forty-five minutes that's been allotted you. Indubitably, you see nothing of the city you've landed in. And to clinch it all, we came back empty-handed more than half the time—way, way more than half. It takes more than one visit to get money out of a potential investor. I would prepare for fifty meetings in the hopes that ten would go well enough that I would be able to wring some money out of five. That was the gig and it was not my first roadshow.

Back in 2010, I had been on the road in Europe with a broker from Goldman Sachs to raise money for a new distressed fund. The banker looked sixteen years old and had about the investment acumen of a teenager as well. He arranged a meeting in Brest, France. Now, I am French—and I had never been to Brest, which is less than four hundred miles from Paris. Brest is no Singapore. There are no Crazy Rich French there. The population is barely one hundred fifty thousand people. What it does have in vast quantities, however, is rain. It rains on average 159 days a year, which prompted this joke from locals: it only rains twice a year in Brest… each time, it lasts six months. Imagine my curiosity when I was told we would meet a prospect in Brest.

Curiosity may not be the right word; I could have told the pubescent banker that no money would come out of our adventure. But off we went, over an hour's flying time from Paris, meaning an entire day spent getting to and back from the meeting on a crappy turboprop. It was, fittingly, pouring. We drove around in the limo and got hopelessly lost. Brest is a picturesque medieval port city on the Atlantic Ocean with a stunning coastline, but all I remember is meandering down a never-ending forest road. Forget investors, there were no buildings. We finally arrived at some kind of commercial facility, completely empty and visibly unfinished. I am not exaggerating; the doors were missing. There was no receptionist, no assistant, not even a janitor. My voice echoed as though I were standing atop a mountain peak in the Alps when I yelled, "Bonjour?" And then out of nowhere came a French gentleman, and we sat down in a room that was empty save for a table and a couple of chairs. He could have been a local fisherman dressed up for church for all I knew. But I gave him my most convincing performance—if ever there was someone to make the good people of Richelieu's historical naval base fork out their riches to invest in distressed bonds, it would be I. Coming out of the meeting, I snorted an imprecation and swore I would shave my head if we ever saw an investment from Brest—and we did not. It was probably one of the safest bets I ever made in my twenty-year career in investing, although one with the least upside.

JUST RICH ENOUGH

Investors love successful people. There is an American tendency to be impressed with somebody because they are rich. They trust that you are going to be good with their money too. Their natural inclination is to want to be part of their success. And who could blame them? "I'm investing with George Soros," I imagine they all would like to say. Why, the fellow whose wealth is over $8 billion, who made $1 billion shorting the pound sterling in 1992, and became known as "the Man Who Broke the Bank of England," you're investing with that chap? Well, seriously.

Yet, you do not want to look too successful and too rich either in front of investors. It is a rather fine line. They don't want to tie their fortunes to a sartorially challenged loser who can't afford anything but polyester and cheap shoes—and trust me, cheap shoes always show. But if I showed up wearing a Tiffany diamond tiara like Lady Gaga at the Oscars, I would almost be signaling that I intended to steal their money rather than invest it. What to tone down and what to amplify truly separates the hedge fund expert from the layman, and the topic stirred more than one shallow but entertaining conversation with Jeff, my right-hand CLO collaborator.

We mostly met institutional investors, meaning people who invest on behalf of others (a pension fund, an insurance company, a family office) as well as consultants who act as intermediaries and advisors to the same groups. Trust me, none was fabulously wealthy, or even stinking rich. They made very decent livings by any reasonable standard but never attained the level of wealth of the people who were supposed to service them, that is, the hedge fund managers. As a rule, the latter are the wealthy and eccentric ones, not the former.

I did meet two fabulously rich, incredibly cool, non-hedge-fund people on the job. Although I didn't mean to imply hedge fund guys could be cool, myself included. I met James Cameron, the movie director. For years I bragged about it, on occasions that I confess were only loosely related to the topic or not at all, to people I knew or not, proudly displaying his cell phone entry in my iPhone contacts. That is, until I showed it to my older brother. "How do you know it's his cell?" he inquired suspiciously. "Have you ever called him?" The truth is, I had not. And after his comment, I never will. I am both anxious that James Cameron could answer, and worried that I have carried a random number for six years. No, the least embarrassing outcome is, if James happens to read these lines, that *he* calls *me*. Anyway, I met James Cameron. Twice. Once in his office, once in mine. I had invested in a company called Panavision, first at a profit in the late '90s and early 2000s. The success did not last. Panavision was a legendary company founded in the '50s, once the leading provider of movie and TV cameras. It commanded over 80 percent market share for decades. Watch any movie or TV show dating before 2000 and chances are that the Panavision credit rolls at the end. Every director, every cinematographer wanted to use their cameras and their lenses, for which the company won more Oscars than Meryl Streep. But the new millennium ushered in the era of reality TV and digital cameras, rendering analog cameras obsolete or measurably less prestigious. The company embarked on a series of disastrous acquisitions, all debt-financed, while at the same time working on developing a digital and a 3D camera. Panavision went from quasi-monopoly domination to heavily threatened by new digital entrants to finally bankrupt, restructuring its balance sheet in 2010. The equity holder, Ron Perelman, relinquished the keys to the debt holders—I was the second largest one and Canyon became an owner of the company and I a board member. In 2009, a little movie called *Avatar*, directed by James Cameron, was released. The first film ever captured in 3D, it utilized two rigged-up cameras that Cameron and his partner Vince Pace conceived. My big idea was to convince them to buy Panavision. It had the brand, it had the R&D (particularly in lenses), it had market presence. But it needed cash.

The first meeting was at their office, Lightstorm Entertainment, headquartered in Santa Monica. There must have been no fewer than fifteen people around the conference table: the partners and myself from Canyon, James Cameron, Vince Pace, and...the rest of them, many of whom young and of the female gender. Who were all these people? I had no idea. Agents, PR reps, bankers, assistants? They didn't say hello to me or utter a single word during our two-hour meeting. I must hand it to my partners, they turned the meeting over to me immediately after we introduced ourselves. Everyone was familiar with Panavision, but I explained the financial details in terms that I was unsure would be understood—leveraged buyout, first-lien and second-lien loans, equitization of debt, out-of-court restructuring. The crowd just stared like I was speaking Na'vi. But let me tell you something about James Cameron. First, he is very tall. That is always a fine starting point in my book. Second, the man apparently can spend four years inventing tall, blue-colored people lost in the jungle, wagging their tails, and two hours dissecting the restructuring of an over-leveraged company. One of the finest minds I have encountered—with Bill Sharpe, naturally. His grasp of my world was as thorough as mine of Pandora was shallow. Plus, he seemed genuinely interested in a deal. And he gave me his business card with his cell phone number, requesting that I follow up with "his people" to discuss merger possibilities. *If I sell that ghost company to James Cameron,* I thought, *I am retiring on the spot.*

It never got past the confidentiality agreement, by which I mean that the agreement did not even get signed. I tried reaching Vince or his representatives for months to no avail. I drove myself nuts trying to move a deal forward. Ten months after the first meeting, an assistant called to schedule a follow-up one. This time, James was coming to Canyon's office. He was still the same tall, wickedly smart man, plus $3 billion in box office revenue—which made him taller. He still seemed interested in the acquisition idea—unless he was just fascinated by me. Unfortunately, it remained an idea and I never saw him again. Panavision continued to sink and abandoned its 3D camera project. I am not bitter. I wish James the absolute best and I hope he is well—after all, I note with a certain concern that he has not released a movie since he last met me.

Speaking of tall and rich men, I introduced Elon Musk at one of our research retreats at the Beverly Hills Hotel, where he spoke twice. It was probably 2011, because he was about to launch the Tesla Model S and the second version of the Falcon 9 rocket, and he was a lot thinner. Whether it is the job or the weed, I would not know since I am neither working nor smoking pot. His speech, in his inimitably casual style, described a professional path focused on solving such issues as nonphysical transactions, solar energy, space travel. I call solving an issue unclogging the toilet. He spoke as if in his family room speaking to a few buddies about sports— we were enthralled. As he explained, low-key, that SpaceX would allow people to sell their possessions and move to Mars to seek a fresh start, everyone in the ballroom wanted to raise their hand and shout, "I'm free Sunday; what about Sunday for a fresh start?" We then all rushed to the valet parking because he had driven up in the spanking-new Model S and hedge fund guys are big on expensive cars (among other expensive things). I am certain that if he had arrived at the hotel in his Falcon rocket, half of Canyon would have wanted to buy a space shuttle for their garage. That's when I asked my husband to put a deposit down for the Model S. I had a feeling that moving to Mars just was not going to fly at my house.

SPAGHETTI AND PACHYDERM

When you get on the road, there are two types of meetings. The first are the courtesy visits, meant to update a prospect or an existing client on business and investing conditions. These usually have a free-flowing, question-and-answer format. Then there are "deal roadshows" meant to sell a specific new fund or product. These are grueling, military-like campaigns spread over a one- or two-week intense trip around the U.S., Asia, or Europe. Four or five meetings a day, a flight in the evening, a few hours of sleep, rinse and repeat.

There is a presentation to go over (usually with the visual help of a pitch book), heavily rehearsed and rigidly followed. It's tedious and repetitive. It is all orchestrated, and not in a Mendelssohn *Midsummer Night's Dream* kind of way. We got the same questions, to which we reacted as if the person had asked something no one before had ever thought to ask, and then we gave the same answers. I made the same jokes, and Jeff—I commend his spirit—guffawed each time. To combat boredom, this admirable colleague, an even-tempered fellow who usually displayed a high level of intelligence and logic, came up with a game that I cannot reasonably describe as making any particular sense. He decided on a mystery word that we had to insert into our presentation, the first one to do so naturally becoming the winner and earning the right to mock, shame, and generally belittle other team members over a period deemed reasonable by him. He sailed over "spaghetti" in a record three minutes, while "pachyderm" was more of a nail-biter.

Not to be upstaged, I tried to add a little piquancy of my own to these trips. Japanese offices usually have hard construction hats lined up on a low shelf of the boardroom (because of the ever-present earthquake threats, I imagine, unless they break into spontaneous wall-plastering as a team-building exercise). One of my skills, which remained unchallenged throughout years of road-shows, was to put a hat on and get photographed with it in the few minutes between our team entering the meeting room and investors pouring in. Mature stuff like that.

We could afford these shenanigans only because we were solidly prepared. Not that any serious manager would brag about being unprepared, but I probably went the extra mile for several reasons. The sure facts are that I am terrible at small talk; I don't know the first thing about sports I do not practice, let alone the ones that involve face painting by fans or foul spitting by players; and I would not go out drinking with the client and would only grudgingly accept dinner. In other words, no amount of schmoozing of mine would ingratiate investors. Only my work would. Lastly, my feeling was that if a male manager makes a mistake, they will remember the mistake. But if a female hedge fund manager makes a mistake, they will remember the woman. It's true. There is evidence[10] that people who are employed in an occupation that is strongly associated with the opposite gender are penalized more harshly for errors. In other words, women who fail in finance would suffer direr consequences than men would for the same failure, and the opposite is true for, say, male nurses. Aside from saluting them for a job infinitely more helpful to society than mine was, I can only recommend my own method: just prepare better.

A finance professor at Stanford recently sent me an even more specific research paper that examined the consequences of misconduct (such as unauthorized trading, churning accounts to generate excess commissions, misrepresenting the risks associated with a financial product, and committing outright fraud) in the financial advisory industry.[11] The results are damning. To begin with, male advisors are twice as likely to commit misconduct than their female peers. But do women get the benefit of the doubt? Hardly. Female advisors are 20 percent more likely to lose their jobs than male advisors after misconduct. Could this corporate behavior be rationally explained by higher female recidivism or graver wrongdoing? In other words, are females punished harder because they don't learn and they cost more? No again. Females face harsher outcomes despite engaging in misconduct that is 20 percent less costly and having a substantially lower propensity toward repeat offenses. And here is the clincher: the gap shrinks for branches with more female managers, meaning a greater number of women in positions of power. No profit-maximization reason can explain these observed results. It is as pure a sexist model as can be. The authors call it "the gender punishment gap."

And so my meeting preparation began long before the first conference call and the first meeting, well in advance of getting on the road at all, with a solid thesis. The thread of the narration came from me, and my team filled in the data and commentaries. Our competitive edge, made into a coherent, salable pitch, essentially went like this: "There are many CLO managers you could choose from. Thank you for considering Canyon today." Now I sounded like an airline flight attendant. "With a Canyon CLO, you are paying the price of a no-thrill, low-fee product, but my team, who will manage and invest on your behalf, is world-class hedge fund material—in other words, we are the smartest people on Wall Street. I am offering to fly you on Singapore Airlines for the price of Southwest."

The pitch was high-end and had to be a white-glove delivery. In that respect, I am a believer in lavishly rehearsing. I wrote out every word, to the comma and exclamation point, and practiced my bit everywhere, in the bathtub, in the gym, and in my car, as I do for all public speaking engagements. Likewise, I insisted that the team learn their parts and rehearse them because, honestly, not every hedge fund analyst has the charisma of Christian Bale in *The Big Short*—even when Christian Bale wears shapeless T-shirts and a glass eye. Come to think of it, Christian Bale as Dick Cheney is probably more charismatic than most of them. We even had a public speaking coach give us a seminar.

Speech preparation is like makeup for French women. It should appear as if there is not any, as if you just woke up, bare-faced and natural. Naturally beautiful, that is, without working at it. The worst is to look like you try too hard. The ideal speech is logical, convincing, flowing, with a hint of spontaneous and nonchalant lightness—even if it is a grind to get there.

BIG IN JAPAN

Meetings are always hard to judge, but there is a special place in my memory for the ones that went dreadfully awry, especially those in Japan and Korea in the first years of trawling for CLO money.

One Korean prospect whom I met half a dozen times, or so it felt, ran the investment fund for the army pension. He always wore sweats of undefined color and shape, and generally looked like a homeless veteran. Even so, he was sharp, engaged, and always seemed interested, even engrossed. But he had never invested, always teasing, never providing. It had been years. At the last meeting, he'd brought a junior analyst, a young puppy who seemed so genuinely happy to be part of things, listening so intently that I thought he might jump up and lick my hand at any moment. I had a good feeling about it all. We were on the verge of something constructive. I really put feeling into my pitch. Then, a dense half an hour into the slides, the junior asked a question, the nature of which pushed me right into despair. Obviously, he had no under-standing of leveraged loans, let alone CLOs. He was blissfully ignorant of my investment topic. It dawned on me that this was no pitch meeting—it was an educational session. I tried to answer his question simply; a few minutes later, he asked me the same one in a different way. So it went for a few rounds until his boss literally told him to shut up (I know because the interpreter translated with a chuckle). I finished the presentation, dispirited, and then we had to move on to our next potential investor and regurgitate the pre-sentation all over again. I never even got even a tiny pity invest-ment from the army pension fund.

The meetings in Japan always seemed to follow a strict pro-tocol. Four or five men would come in and present their business cards, then we all would smile, bow, and sit down. In more than eight years of meeting investors in Japan, I met just one female executive. I should remember her name, but shame on me, I do not. She was very petite, or maybe she looked that way because of where she sat. Let me explain.

On that occasion, my Canyon team had been demoted from a meeting room to a closet-size space that looked as inviting as the waiting room of a free health clinic. My two colleagues and I were crammed onto a three-seat leather sofa. The Japanese team entered and, silently, as naturally as if it were the law of Darwin, the men took the two armchairs while the woman sat on a little stool. She had a pile of printouts and notes precariously stacked on her lap. She had obviously studied because she asked specific and on-point questions about our CLO deals. She was the best—the only—prepared member of the Japanese team in the room. And she was sitting on a footrest.

I must confess that this unfortunate seating arrangement was the result of my own behavior as it were. First, I admit that I have an ego of a certain size. I lose patience easily. I send emails too quickly. Honestly, I can occasionally be rather reasonable, but pay close attention or you may miss it.

Here is what happened. This Japanese company was an early investor in our CLO bonds that had required, about a year earlier, their approval for a change in terms. The change was technical in nature and inconsequential, yet they refused to give their approval unless we paid them a fee. I declined to pay but insisted they approve the change, explaining that they would not be worse off and would do me a solid, and vaguely threatening that they could need a favor back someday, somewhere. Looking over my shoulder as I composed this response, Jeff wisely advised me to back down. I pressed "Send" anyway. Their next email read something like, "You asked some rule changes and before we to you no said. Therefore we please you do not ever ask again."

Now, when no one bothers to check the grammar of a message in English, you must appreciate that this is serious business.

I knew, because I had seen such an imperative command before, in the public toilet of a Kyoto restaurant to be specific. It read, "Attention. This toilet is automatic. This toilet automatically drains water. Please push the button when you do not drift. Please do not use except when toileting paper." As if the "please" fooled anyone.

As we entered the lobby in Tokyo and got into the elevator for the in-person meeting, our salesperson from Goldman Sachs, a young and prim fellow who was acting as the intermediary between the investors and my firm, politely pulled me aside. He coldly informed me that the investors were vexed. So displeased in fact, that they had transferred the meeting to a junior team to lead, in a closet, without proper seating—which was rough on their own analysts, but who was I to judge? My marching orders were to apologize immediately as an introduction, in a manner of my choosing.

It isn't simple to beat your ego into submission in the span of two elevator floors in order to ask strangers for forgiveness of wrongdoing you believe you did not commit, sandwiched between two colleagues on a springless sofa. But thus it was that I launched into a very personal rendition of Mishima's hara-kiri mixed with Tom Hanks's emotionally charged apology to his volleyball in *Cast Away* ("I'm sorry, Wilson! I'm sorry!")

I am not one to brag, but Jeff swore that the performance was Oscar-worthy. However, after thanking my agent, my producer, and my makeup artist, I must observe that apologizing is something women are generally better at than men are. It comes naturally to us; we spend our lives saying it.

"Sorry, I didn't hear you, you were saying...?"

"I'm sorry, where is the bathroom?"

"Apologies for interrupting, but may I?"

We are always sorry about this, that, or the other because, at least according to a study published in *Psychological Science* in

2010, women have a lower threshold definition of which offenses require an apology.

Now, usually women's magazines, blogs, self-help books, and other similarly ego-sapping literature recommend that we women apologize less (who would have thought of that?). I stick to my apologies, however, and use them abundantly, especially when selling to men. I get good money out of it.

So good, in fact, that Japan turned out to be my biggest success as a marketer. I honestly don't remember if we ever clawed back that initially discontented bank, but I never cared because every CLO deal we issued after the initial one in 2012 had at least one significant group of Japanese investors. Some started investing with my CLO team before expanding into investing in the Canyon hedge fund. My popularity was such that I was invited to give a speech to important Japanese clients, this time in a large and airy boardroom, and attendance was by invitation only. Inevitably, one client asked the head of Canyon's Japanese office, "What does Dominique look like?" He answered deadpan and quick as a whip, "Julia Roberts."

Now, I must say, regretfully, that there was some marketing license taken, but this fellow is a consummate salesperson who could sell ice to Inuit people. Then again, the conference setup baffled me. I was to give my speech in English, during which my Japanese colleague would translate, word for word, slide by slide. Why, pray, did they need me at all if they did not understand English? Why not have my Japanese colleague just make the presentation? I guess they really wanted to meet Julia Roberts.

MARRIED WITH CHILDREN

While I was never a victim of active sexism, as I discussed previously, I did at times feel very isolated on the job. Whom could I talk to if I felt, rightly or wrongly, that my ideas were underinvested in because I was a woman? I was the sole woman in the investment meetings at Canyon, and in almost all the large restructuring or bankruptcy committees I ever participated in or led, among them, the U.S. airlines, DynCorp, Brookstone, Travelport, Eagle Bulk Shipping…the list goes on. It is not always easy to be heard in such a scenario.

Then there were the times when the frontier between mild prejudice and flat-out chauvinism got crossed. One such time was a kickoff meeting with our lead equity investor in New York for my first CLO as the head of the business. We sat in an immense and dark conference room with a hollow-square seating arrangement. The setup felt unusually formal for people meant to become deal partners for ten years. When we came to discuss the value of having a "debt lock" (meaning a guaranteed issuance of a tranche of debt at a certain interest rate), the sixty-something-year-old European CFO snorted that this guarantee was worthless.

"It isn't," I objected. "It's an option that's currently out of the money, but an option is never worthless before maturity." What I meant is that even if the current price of the underlying security (a stock, interest rate, currency, or commodity) is below the price at which the option allows one to buy it, as long as there is time until the option expires, there is economic value. Imagine you had the option, if you so desired, to be a passenger on the first manned spaceship to Mars if it launched before 2030. Would that potential seat be worthless simply because no such rocket exists now? It would not, since space travel might evolve in the next decade. The passage of time is a commodity that has a price in finance.

Hence, my response was not a subjective or flippant comment on my part. It was finance 101.

That's when the CFO responded with this mystifying repartee, and I quote, "You are a woman. I am a man. Therefore, we are not going to continue this debate."

I had to snap my jaw back in place with my fingers before continuing the debate along the line of reason despite his injunction. Twice more, he reiterated his man-woman ultimatum with the added disgrace of raising his right hand high in the air in a gesture to stop me. I turned to my team (all men), who were dead silent, studiously absorbed in taking notes. A conundrum indeed. Should they speak up on my behalf, thereby implying that I needed the support of men actually working for me? Or should they pretend they did not have a dog in this fight? I would have preferred they diplomatically explained that two Nobel Prize-winning men (Myron Scholes and Robert Merton) had decades ago developed the option pricing theory I was invoking and that, if I may use one of my favorite expressions, I was right.

I let it go. I did not have a choice as that was the only expected business behavior. We had to make our way to dinner. I seriously considered going back to the hotel room to have a strong drink or a good cry, but Jeff, unflappably cool and usually able to talk me off the ledge, convinced me to swallow my pride. "He's an alcoholic," Jeff said. "Stick around. You'll outlive him." He died of cirrhosis of the liver years ago, not that I would ever mention this as some type of karmic revenge.

Before we leave this rather dispiriting amble down memory lane, a special shout-out to a Japanese team who flew into Canyon's office to conduct due diligence for a potential CLO investment. They began by asking me what time I got to work (6:30 a.m. at the latest), what time I left for the day (6:00 p.m. at the earliest) and a few other rather innocuous work-ethic questions. It started getting interesting when they inquired how old I was, whether I was single or married, and if I had children (my responses: old enough, married, two children). Then they asked if I planned to have more children. "Well," I said helpfully, "it depends. How many would you like me to bear?" They answered, their manner entirely dead-pan, that two children are the maximum a woman can have without jeopardizing her workload. "Two," I said, "You got it. But if you revise to three, kindly let me know before the end of the meeting and I'll get on it tonight. I'm dedicated like that."

Somehow, they invested anyway.

CHAPTER 13

THE OUTSIDER HAS LEFT THE BUILDING

Partner was the highest level I could achieve at the firm, barring becoming the CEO if one of the founding partners retired—and that seemed highly unlikely. Hedge fund owners have a way of lingering, you see. Leon Cooperman, founder of Omega Advisors, retired last year, turning his fund into a family office. "I don't want to spend the rest of my life chasing the S&P 500," he said, "I know when to fold 'em." Really? He was seventy-five years old; he might have folded a smidge earlier, if he was being honest about his motivations. It's not exactly the action of a sage to quit 1.1 years before the average American male croaks.

When I became a partner, my perspective changed somewhat. I had reached the top; now what? What was the right benchmark of progression and success? Some kind of Bridget Jones's diary tracking bonus, title, and portfolio size instead of cigarettes, pounds, and rear-end size? I entered the business because I fell in love with the creativity of investing, the discoveries, and the competitive spirit. After checking the two boxes of status and financial well-being, what else was there? Leadership? Ownership? Commitment? Fulfillment? It became tougher to answer, or rather, it became trickier to come up with truthful answers rather than forced rationalization.

THE DODD–FRANK CONUNDRUM

In 2016, regulations around securitization product issuance changed, calling for a serious overhaul of CLO structures, among others. We had surmised that a transformation was coming after the financial crisis of 2008. It arrived in 2010 in the form of the Dodd–Frank Wall Street Reform and Consumer Protection Act. A massive piece of legislation, Dodd–Frank was passed under the Obama administration with the goal of avoiding a repeat of the excessive risks taken in the financial industry. Among the many new rules was a policy for securitizations that obligated the entity that creates them to maintain a significant ownership interest over the life of the vehicles (specifically, 5 percent of the capital structure, which is a significant sum for the average $500 million deal). The idea was for the entity that issues a deal (bank, hedge fund, insurance) to have skin in the game and feel as much pain as investors if the deal crashes. Otherwise, the issuer could build a house of paper on top of an earthquake zone, get paid a structuring fee, sell it all to unsuspecting investors while retaining no economic interest, and wash its hands of the mess if the house crumbled. They called it the risk retention rule.

CLOs were included in the policy, a deeply controversial decision. Unlike mortgage securitizations, CLOs had neither caused nor amplified the crisis, nor had they systematically failed or even performed poorly. In fact, they had behaved splendidly in the form of double-digit returns if you held on throughout and past the 2008 crisis. Nevertheless, they were painted with the same brush as other securitization products and got the same Dodd–Frank treatment.

Think of the practical consequence of the new rule as follows: before 2016, in order to issue a $500 million deal, a CLO manager needed talented people to raise the funds; an investment team, of course; and also marketing, accounting, legal, and compliance staff. After 2016, a CLO manager needed that *plus* $25 million of capital (5 percent of the assets of the deal). The new rules transformed a low-fee, capital-light business into a low-fee, capital-intensive one, weeding out small managers and killing some of the economics.

Although the federal law was enacted in 2010, it took effect in 2016. The interim grace period was so that loan trading associations, lawyers, bankers, and practitioners could comment, in the form of white papers, and to give time for the industry to adapt. By 2016, all new CLOs would have to comply with the risk retention rule.

I did not want to wait. It was critical to show that Canyon was ahead of the game. I needed to be first in reimagining the structure of the business and taking to market a new financing solution, showing that we were creative, resourceful, and committed to the business and to our investors. With help from our marketing team, outside legal counsel, and bankers, as well as the support of the founding partners, I succeeded in structuring and marketing a special-purpose equity fund to comply with the Dodd–Frank regulation while keeping the CLO's integrity and profitability. It looked like a private equity fund, where outside investors pool their money to buy a newly formed capitalized manager vehicle (CMV), which in turns retains the equity of CLOs issued by Canyon. In essence, the CMV retains part of the risk, which accommodated Dodd–Frank, but it was not capitalized with money from Canyon, which accommodated us.

I was, and still am, immensely proud of the concept. Naturally, being a solution provider is in the nature of a distressed hedge fund like Canyon. We invested in troubled companies on the edge of, in, or coming out of bankruptcy, which means various degrees of messiness in the business, the balance sheet, the capital structure, or all three. The goal is to turn a problem into an opportunity. The CMV idea was a variation on that theme, not a company in trouble that needed an ingenious restructuring, but a business in transition that required a new solution. I can't paint, I can't dance, I can't sing (I am an outstanding whistler, although that skill is rarely requested), but in finance, I found a deeply creative outlet. We spent countless hours figuring out the ugly legal plumbing of where and when the money would come in and the fees that would be paid, then drafting the legal documents and making it all ironclad.

ONE HECKUVA EPITAPH

I was as delighted with the execution as with the theory of the CMV. My idea was to raise $150 million, which led to another volley of "Why so small?" "Why not more?" from the partners. My reasons were speed and, to some degree, shrewdness. Call me cagey, but I suspected that regulations would change again. I wanted to raise enough money for four deals but not so much that I, and the investors, would be stuck in a vehicle that was no longer the best mousetrap.

Or maybe it was just this deuced woman thing again. I don't always have to go big or go home, as the testosterone-laden saying goes. I am all for taking risks—as long as they pay. It turns out that this may very well be a feminine peculiarity. In 2015, Financial Skills (founded by ex-Merrill Lynch traders) studied 326 junior traders. My favorite excerpt comes from the COO, David Hesketh: "We found that men take more risk than women. That would be fine if they also made more money—but they don't." The results showed that female traders lost less money than men did, while—

mark this—men transgressed specified trading limits two and a half times more often.

Yet it still does not compute. Take Paul Tudor Jones (referenced before with the oh-so-cute idea of carving three islands into his initials because no one could stop him). At an industry conference in 2013, he made this fuckwit comment: "You will never see as many great women investors or traders as men. Period. End of story." He continued, "I can think of two [women] that actually started E. F. Hutton with me. Within four years, by 1980, right when I was getting ready to launch my company, they both got married. Then they both had—which in my mind is as big of a killer as divorce is—they both had children.

"And as soon as that baby's lips touched that girl's bosom, forget it. Every single investment idea, every desire to understand what's going to make this go up or go down is going to be over-whelmed by the most beautiful experience, which a man will never share, about a mode of connection between that mother and that baby. I just see it happen over and over. I am talking about trading, not managing."

I could, if I wanted, paraphrase this to, "As soon as a male trader sees boobs bigger than his head, every investment idea is overwhelmed by the desire to understand what's going to make his thing go up." But I am not like that.

Thankfully, my partners were converts to the seemingly atypical way of thinking known as gender equality and were confident in my abilities to trade, manage, and market. I got on the road with their blessing. As for raising money, I was the messiah of Canyon CLO. The marketing team screened for promising clients and sent us on our way, but I decided on the message and directed the meetings.

Sometimes they sent me far, far away—to the South. I bet no one would ever mistake me for a Southern girl, but Ole Miss holds a special place in my heart because the University of Mississippi was our first sizable CMV investor. I hereby salute and thank them. The endowment had around $500 million at the time, which is exceedingly small compared to Yale, Harvard, or Stanford, and made them a somewhat unlikely candidate for an innovative financial product. To get to Oxford, Mississippi, from New York took two planes and a two-hour car ride. I recollected my meeting in Brest with a sense of foreboding.

A cheery woman greeted us with a "Hi, y'all" before we entered the board of directors meeting, and then uttered words that I didn't recognize as coming from the Oxford dictionary. Twenty-something board members, more than a majority of them white men, sat studiously, waiting for my presentation. The thought crossed my mind that sending a French woman and a Chinese American man to get Ole Miss as an investor was slightly off strategically. I could not tell their level of investing proficiency. Their familiarity with the CLO product was, unsurprisingly, low, but they were spectacularly open, engaged, and *fun* to pitch to. I may have tried a few "y'alls" of my own by the end of the meeting.

The way back to Los Angeles was exhausting. I had started the day around five in the morning and finally reached home around midnight, when a text crossed my phone: Ole Miss was in for our largest order so far. "Life is like a box of chocolates…you never know what you're gonna get." And before anyone remarks that Forrest Gump is from Alabama, it is close enough to Mississippi for a Parisian girl.

Thus, my partners were rewarded for their trust. I raised the fund in three months, a capital-raise blitzkrieg; closed it in mid-2015, well ahead of the implementation of Dodd–Frank; and lost eight pounds, or roughly 7 percent of my total weight, in the process. Nothing ever comes free.

When I finally departed the industry, *Creditflux*, the CLO industry rag, reported: "Mielle had been at Canyon since 1998 and is understood to have been the longest serving partner at the firm upon her departure. One of her biggest accomplishments was spearheading the formation of a capitalized manager vehicle— Canyon CLO Advisors—back in 2015. This is believed to be the first CMV in the market and it has been used by Canyon to launch three dual-compliant US CLOs."

This will be my epitaph: "Here lies Dominique Mielle, beloved wife, mother, and friend, creator of the first CMV."

In the end, the irony of all ironies is that this specific structure has become useless. The application of Dodd–Frank to CLOs was overturned in 2018 under the Trump administration. Such is the nature of finance, always evolving. However, although the CMV was designed in response to the risk retention rule, it turned out to be a highly efficient way to raise capital and invest equity. After the elimination of the rule and my leadership at Canyon, the CMV is still the vehicle that Canyon uses to raise capital. It proved resilient, profitable, and truly innovative.

THE TRUMP BUMP…TO SEXISM

The election of Donald Trump as president of the United States in November 2016 caused me a great deal of discomfort. I mention this not coincidentally. I became more acutely aware of how out of place I was. There were more instances of sexism after the Trump election, as if men had been granted a license. Some were harmless but rather annoyingly petulant, like one heated conversation I recall with a portfolio manager, about a trade we disagreed on, which went like this:

Me: "This trade is bad; you should have discussed with me ahead of time."

Him: "You're too emotional right now, so we can't have a conversation."

Me, with unemotional contempt: "I'm not emotional. I'm mad as hell. Can you tell the difference?"

And honestly, there really is one. I heard the emotional word often on Wall Street, generally as a catchall shut-up-now tool against women, almost used synonymously with hysterical (not meant in a ha-ha way). Let's be clear, hysterical is by definition a sexist attribute and one cannot justify its use by arguing that it is a gender-neutral insult. Men cannot be called hysterical, for the good reason that the etymology of the word is "uterus." Hysteria, or being hysterical, was believed, in the nineteenth century, to be a neurotic condition peculiar to women and thought to be caused by a dysfunction of the uterus. *That* I remember vividly from Freud and the Psychopathology of Everyday Life at HEC Paris. This type of weaponizing language comes right out of insecurity.

Then there were the real outbursts of moronic speech. Why, just a few months ago, Ken Fisher, CEO of Fisher Investments, which manages $112 billion in assets, was interviewed at the Tiburon CEO Summit conference in San Francisco, and besides discussing genitalia (who doesn't at such events?), declared gamely that winning clients is like "trying to get into a girl's pants." What a respectable CEO. The only clients he deserves are escort services, not serious institutional investors.

As it happened, on the eve of the presidential election, I was in Japan meeting CLO investors with my team. In our private car the day before, one of the analysts asked me—in front of the entire team, including the head of our Japanese office and our outside brokers—"If Clinton loses, will you break down in pieces and start crying in the meeting?" Now, correct me if I am indelicate, but would anyone ask a man if he'd break down and cry *in a meeting* after a political result? By the second time he made the comment, I was (as I have indicated I tend to become in these types of situations) pissed. He later explained it as a silly joke to make light of the situation. But here is where I become obtuse. If it was a joke, how come I, the boss, was not laughing?

That night, Jeff and I watched the election results on television in a plush suite of the Peninsula Tokyo hotel. I was convinced of a Clinton victory. As we watched state after state fall into the Trump category, I still held hopes that she could win, calculating her odds of making it. He finally declared, "Let's call it. It's time to take the patient off life support."

I was still incredulous. "Seriously, you think she lost?"

Jeff turned to me with a warm, comforting look of compassion and nodded. "Yes, it's done. It's over. Finito, the end."

After CNN announced the final result, we split. He returned to his hotel room. I went out for a long walk in in the dark and the drizzling rain.

When I got back, I headed right for the elevator to the twenty-fourth floor. Peter: The Bar is a sleek space with shiny silver metal trees, purple mood lights, and a panoramic view of the Imperial Palace. I had two stiff drinks alone. It had never happened before and has never happened since. I am pretty small. Two drinks are a lot.

That night, the S&P futures nose-dived seven hundred points. I went back to my hotel room and called the trader several times overnight to cover some short index positions. By the time I woke up the next day, however, the U.S. market had rebounded and closed almost flat.

I had to figure out what message to convey to investors in the following days' meetings. They wanted to hear about market and interest rate predictions, economic scenarios, and regulatory changes. I needed to strike a balance between my gloomy feeling and the professional obligation to be constructive and opportunist. What I wished to say was, "This is so depressing that I probably should be in the psych ward." What I had to sell was, *what a unique investing opportunity indeed...*

Granted, over the twenty years I had toiled in the hedge fund industry, the U.S. had more Republican presidential years than not. Many people in the hedge fund world are traditional Republicans who want less government, fewer taxes, and are generally fiscally conservative. Few, like George Soros and Tom Steyer, are notorious Democrats—very few. But this was different.

For one thing, all extreme-right politicians look the same these days. Namely, they have a turkey neck. Lindsey Graham: turkey neck. Mitch McConnell, Ted Cruz, Donald Trump: turkey necks. And watch, it is going global: Boris Johnson, Jair Bolsonaro? Turkey necks. Understandably, part of it is the natural upshot of being old and fat, but I still find it somewhat uncanny. Do they screen for it? If they do, no wonder Macron, Trudeau, and Obama had to be on the left.

More to the point, do you remember when Trump attacked the federal judge who was presiding over the lawsuit against his university? Judge Gonzalo Curiel was born in the U.S. and is an American citizen. His *parents* were Mexican. Yet Trump suggested that the judge would be biased against him because of his Mexican heritage. Now, that is the very definition of racism—to assert that someone is incompetent not because of who he is or what he does, but exclusively due to his ethnicity. My children squarely fall into this category: American citizens with a Mexican father.

Both my husband and I are immigrants. We felt the moral assault of this new presidency head-on. The Trump election marked the first time I seriously considered quitting finance entirely.

Don't get me wrong, I was just as ambitious and hungry as the next guy, maybe more so, but not ambitious at the expense of my beliefs. Over the next year, the market roared—and it has not stopped since. From November 2016 to the end of that year, it closed up 3.4 percent and continued rising throughout 2017. How do you rejoice in making money while feeling sick at the people running the country? I discovered how many colleagues and professional acquaintances had voted for Trump and approved his plans for lower taxes and infrastructure investments (the latter has not been done at the time of this writing and the former was a disaster for California residents) while ignoring his social agenda and personal views. Going to the office became a drag. Thinking about the economy, a downer.

Looking at the market depressed me when it went *up* because it felt like a validation of the administration. I caught myself wishing it would tank. There is no denying that rooting for your own destruction and failure is not exactly the right frame of mind for a good investor. I thought of Walt Whitman's quote, "I have nothing to do with this system, not even what is necessary to oppose it."

The thought of leaving matured and solidified.

THAT'S THAT

If there is any industry where you might find young retirees, it's definitely the hedge fund industry. Relative to the population at large, to retire in your fifties, or even forties for some (me included), is noticeably young. I was not the first one to retire nor the youngest. As I mentioned, the head of research had left in 2012, after which we didn't have a senior-level departure until 2016. Then they happened in rapid succession. In the fall of 2016, one of the most prominent and successful partners left. Then in December, Jeff retired. In March 2017, so did another partner.

Why do senior employees quit in a hedge fund? I hate to speak for others, but since it has never stopped me, I see no reason to stop now. It's usually because they don't want to work for others anymore and they have the luxurious financial freedom to just resign. They have produced decades of returns for investors and general partners, and yet they are not the owners of the firm (sometimes they do not even own their track record). The owners of the firm, or founders, depend on the senior managers for profits and recognition of the firm. Their self-sufficiency is only apparent.

Over time, the senior portfolio managers become more conscious of their self-worth through the transformative effects of their labor.

At this point, if you have recognized Hegel's master-slave dialectic, have a good laugh with me. Most hedge fund guys have never studied philosophy and would assume that Schopenhauer is a brand of artisan beer. I am only speculating here.

It surprised me how many colleagues and working folks, upon the news of my retirement, made the quasi-theatrical response that they were working on enthralling deals, were immeasurably successful, and could not conceive of doing nothing with their lives. My message was, and still is, always the same: I am not selling anything. You want to work, go ahead and please yourself.

For me, it was enough. I had reached the top and I staunchly intended to leave at the top—on an up year, as a partner in a successful and respected firm, and with a thriving securitization business.

A friend of mine, a wickedly smart New York bankruptcy lawyer, had once told me the story of an acquaintance, a corporate lawyer of some forty years at the same firm. One evening, the fellow finished the brief he was writing, put his pen down, and stacked his papers neatly on the desk before turning to his secretary. "Well," he said, "that's that," and walked out of the office forever.

In this succinct behavior lay a poetic efficiency, a graceful whim that was deeply pleasing.

CHAPTER 14

THE END OF AN ERA

Before the 2016 election, my husband and I had both entertained the prospect of moving to another country. Now those plans felt more urgent. I wanted to move to Singapore. My husband favored Chile. The kids thought we had gone bonkers, somewhat rightfully, considering that we had never even visited those places together. We settled for Paris, if one can think of moving to Paris as settling. It was a logical choice. We had an apartment already and my mother was sick. We decided to move for a year because it sounded less scary and definitive, particularly to teenagers who were as interested in moving as a hibernating bear might be.

I told the founding partners that I would be wrapping up my work around Easter of 2017. They asked me kindly to continue working from Paris until at least the end of the year. We moved in August 2017, and while I relinquished all my hedge fund activity, a $3 billion portfolio, I continued to lead and manage the CLO business from abroad. We unsuccessfully explored different structures under which I could continue with Canyon. On January 1, 2018, I parted ways with Canyon. There was no celebration, no balloons; there was no cake and no goodbye. I never stepped into the office again. My twenty-year tenure in the industry was over, and so was—and I do not want you to read any causation into this—the golden age of hedge funds.

THE BLINDERS COME OFF

It is always tempting to connect the end of something personal with the end of something global. I can back this one up, though, from the end of the growth phase to the widespread decline in fees.

Over the last two years, legendary figures with decades-long records of producing remarkable returns, such as David Tepper, Leon Cooperman, and John Paulson, have turned their funds into family offices (which means all the money from outside investors is returned, leaving only the funds of the owner). By managing only their personal fortune, these hedge funds are, in essence, closing. Stan Druckenmiller said in June 2019, "The hedge fund industry is in need of a major shake-out. There's probably five to ten people, women and men, who are worth more than their fees now. There are going to be superstars, but we need to get back to maybe two hundred or three hundred from four thousand funds." (Note: the number is closer to fourteen thousand.)

When David Tepper says that it's time to fold, you know that the business is in a rough spot. Tepper started Appaloosa in 1993 with $57 million and produced annualized returns of about 25 percent over a sixteen-year period. He is considered one of the sharpest traders of the last thirty years. As of today, the fund manages around $13 billion. "The media says that hedge funds are the new masters of the universe," Tepper said back in 2006. "We're just a bunch of schmucks."

Smart and simpatico.

WHEN SIZE MATTERS

To be perfectly honest, the fees we charged didn't trouble me for most of my career. These fees paid my bonus, you see. However, once I convinced myself that we could no longer deliver on the promise made for that compensation, they started becoming bothersome. The bargain we had struck at the outset was simple: we would outperform the market on a consistent basis—be it the stock or the high-yield market or whatever index of your choosing. And we did for a great number of years.

That was not the case anymore, not in a sufficiently systematic or persistent way. So what were we selling? Or rather, was the product I sold priced correctly?

I am not trying to be righteous. I do not pretend to a higher morality. If an industry is not controlled by the government, then what am I asking for? That hedge funds self-regulate their fees based on some vague notion of fairness or social equality? You would be hard pressed to find such an incongruous notion on Wall Street. If overly hefty fees are part of the industry inner workings, and customers continue to flock in droves, who am I to ask to stop the gravy train?

I was not asking anything. I just did not want to be part of it anymore.

That said, in the last ten years, investors have, in fact, clamored for lower fees…albeit at a glacial pace. But this macro trend will continue. Part of it is investors realizing that the fees are too high for the performance, and part of it is the hedge fund industry maturing. As in any industry, when competition builds up, prices usually level off.

Initially, the structure of hedge fund compensation made eminent sense. The management fee, calculated as a percentage of assets, was supposed to cover the cost of running the business. The bigger the fund, the more assets it manages, and the more costs need to be covered. The performance fee was supposed to incentivize the fund to produce the highest returns while aligning its interest with those of investors.

The flaw in this method is that hedge fund expenses do not grow linearly with the growth in assets. When I started in 1998, Canyon managed $500 million in assets with six investment professionals and another six people in the administration and back office. Fast-forward to 2018. Canyon managed about $25 billion in assets, the firm grew fiftyfold, and so did, mathematically, its management fee. However, we were an investment team of only thirty and a total staff of 240. In other words, costs had increased only fivefold in the investment staff—the lion's share of a hedge fund's expenses—and thirty-fivefold in the back office. Yet investors were paying *fifty* times more in management fees.

This fee structure led to a reversal in objective in the hedge fund industry. Instead of pursuing return, it pursued size. Indeed, before the Global Financial Crisis, the aggregate performance fee of the industry was much larger than the management fee. Thereafter, it was the other way around as the management fee dwarfed the performance fee.

As I have argued throughout, the bigger a hedge fund gets, the less nimble it becomes and the less likely it is to outperform the market. The same opinion has been publicly voiced by several legendary investors in different markets. In 2016, speaking at the Milken Institute conference, Steve Cohen of Point72 declared that there were "too many players out there trying to do similar strategies." Dan Loeb wrote in his investment letter the same year that we were "in the first innings of a washout in hedge funds and certain strategies." Since then, the industry has added almost $1 trillion in assets. A superior intuition tells me, however, that both investors referred to the demise and shortcomings of others—their own funds would continue to grow and thrive.

And it shows in the numbers. Not to be fastidiously historical, but from 1998 to 2008, hedge funds beat the S&P in seven out of eleven years, according to the Callan Institute periodic return tables. After 2008, they beat the index...once (in 2018, by 1.1 percent). Yes, for ten out of the past eleven years, the S&P has outperformed hedge funds, not by a little, but by a whopping 9.4 percent. And I suspect that the poor showing of the hedge fund index is understated because it likely has a survival bias—meaning that the worst-performing hedge funds go out of business and are not counted in ensuing years. The studies also agree. A 2018 paper by researchers at Loyola Marymount and Purdue universities ("Size, Age, and the Performance Life Cycle of Hedge Funds") states, "Our results suggest that fund growth over time drives performance declines over a hedge fund's life cycle and that performance persistence is more achievable when funds stay small." The same goes for the industry in aggregate. As it grew in scale, it lost the ability to deliver.

I came upon a fascinating study by Marco Avellaneda, director of the division of financial mathematics at the Courant Institute at New York University, and Paul Besson, head of quantitative research at Euronext, who presciently asked, back in 2005, "Hedge funds: how big is big?" The first concept they introduce is that of capacity, that is, the total amount of money that can be put to work with a given manager or strategy without negatively affecting performance. They corroborate my experience that some strategies (currency trading, for example) have greater capacity than others (distressed investing, in my case), and consequently that investors, all things being equal, should prefer deep capacity rather than niche strategies.

The problem then becomes whether hedge funds can deliver outsized risk-adjusted returns in markets that are highly liquid and efficient. His answer is that they can, to the extent that they offer superior investment skills. And since above-average skills are, by definition, in limited supply as money (i.e., demand for skills) pours into the hedge fund industry, it begins funding managers whose skills "are not superior to those that are needed for index investing." Here, academia poetically meets practitioners. Mr. Cohen succinctly remarked in the same panel that "talent is very thin" and eloquently added that he was "blown away by the lack of talent."

And so comes the point at which hedge funds are too large to beat the market. Professors Avellaneda and Besson use a linear regression to study the marginal return of a dollar invested at any given hedge fund size. As expected, the line is well fitted and downward sloping, meaning that returns diminish as assets increase. Avellaneda and Besson insightfully extrapolate that the hedge fund industry will no longer outperform the S&P 500 past $2 trillion in size. The industry first reached $2.3 trillion in 2008 (dipping for two years after the Global Financial Crisis before ramping back up), precisely the year that started the streak of ten-out-of-eleven-year underperformance. We are at $3.3 trillion today. Go figure.

"Why does money keep pouring into an asset class that demonstrably can be shown to underperform?" I asked the chief investment officer of a large university endowment.

"Well," he answered, it is "akin to asking a large group of people to raise their hands if they believe they have below-average intelligence." Whenever there is wide dispersion in results, every CIO believes they are in the top half *and* they can pick the winners. Now, it would be easy to demonstrate that none of them have been, or will ever be, persistently overperforming. Even David Swensen at Yale had some real doozy years. But here is the clincher: every CIO is highly motivated to at least *try* to pick a hedge fund, and here is why.

"In an investment committee meeting a year or so ago," the veteran CIO recalled, "one of the committee members asked why we had zero low-cost index managers [passive managers, whose portfolios only mirror an index like the S&P 500 or Nasdaq, or the Barclays U.S. Corporate High Yield Total Return Index] in the portfolio. I hesitated for a moment, then told the truth: I get paid to beat the indices. The easiest way to ensure that I *don't* get paid is to invest in an indexed fund—because by definition, once subtracting the fees imposed by the manager, I will underperform the index. So even if 80 percent of active managers underperformed this year, I would still be compelled to try to pick the winners. With venture capital and hedge funds, you are basically buying a lottery ticket. It's like the TV commercials—somebody is going to win, so I may as well play the game, since I know that I can't win if I don't play. And hence, we give the money to the highly paid hedge fund wizards who are much smarter than we are and magically turn 5 percent returns into 10 percent returns. Except, that it's not magic…it's just taking more risk with the false hope that the magicians know how to see into the future, wave their wands, and sell everything right before the crash (or even better, get short). Occasionally, one of the magicians gets lucky and makes a career out of it. Look at John Paulson—he mimicked one trade in size and made a lot of money for his clients. For the next twelve years, the only people who made money were John Paulson and his employees."

John Paulson is known for his genius negative views on real estate values before 2008, which he expressed in his fund through giant short positions in leveraged bonds backed by U.S. residential property. He is said to have earned $4 billion from the trade—personally. To be fair, Paulson repeated his profit feast in 2010 by speculating on gold, supposedly earning $5 billion in the investment. But then the wind turned. His performance became sketchy at best, with a whopping negative 51 percent return in 2011, followed by negative 14 percent in 2012, and down double digits each year from 2015 to 2017. And in July 2020, Paulson called it quits, his fund having dwindled from a peak of $38 billion in assets in 2011 to $10 billion in 2020, most of it his own money. The poor man is turning his business into a family office.

Still, I asked, "Why aren't investors at least moving to an allocation mix of some index and some hedge funds?"

"Again," said the CIO, "the brutal reasons are reputational perception and financial incentive. Over some periods of time (though not recently), active management does beat indexing. Who wants to be underperforming with a simple index strategy when all the smart people are making money hand over fist with private equity and hedge funds? Perhaps even more importantly, who is going to pay me a ridiculous amount of money (at least compared to the mortal world) to manage a simple index? So, the industry participants all continue to dance—pretending that they are adding value and hoping they can make a bunch of money before the next blowup—at which point they will be well under their high-water mark, will shut down (or get fired), and pop up somewhere else in a year or two to start the dance all over again. And lucky for us—hope springs eternal." It must be said that I had asked for a candid answer.

If you do not trust academics and anecdotes from the investing side, there's always Steve Cohen of SAC, a man that no one would accuse of being coy or underselling anything. "We are not going to generate those larger numbers now that we are bigger," he said, back in a 2010 *Vanity Fair* interview. "We're a mature business in a mature industry. When I was generating those big returns, you know, it was 'What's a hedge fund?' We were so much smaller. Now, we're bigger. Math applies. Having said that, I can make a nice living here, which is not a bad place to be in life."

I would never deny a nice living to a fellow hedge fund manager.

INSTITUTIONALIZED SEXISM

Another seismic shift has taken place in hedge funds, the relative importance of hedge fund personnel. From the very first day, the core of the business, the engine that made it run, was the investment team, that is, the portfolio managers, the analysts, and the traders. They are the only profit center of a hedge fund; everyone else is a cost. They are the geniuses, the smartest guys in the room, and consequently the billionaires in the making or already made.

However, now that large hedge fund managers are generally failing to achieve what they are paid for, that is, consistently outperforming the market, what gives? Note that *consistently* is the key word, or, if you would rather use a statistical term, persistence of results. Only *some* of them beat the market and only *sometimes*.

Investors are no longer investing in large funds because of the investment professionals—in fact, they are investing despite them. They are attracted by behemoth funds because it's worked so far (how could those funds be large if it had not?); because of groupthink, from peer recommendations to consultants' endorsements; because of fear of missing out; and because of a good pitch and solid reputation. In other words, they invest because of the marketing, not the investing.

Yet the money still goes to the investing group. I believe that my bonus was considerably higher than that of the cohead of marketing, the only other female partner at Canyon during my tenure. The business has turned into an asset-gathering exercise, creating new products (like a CLO fund), designing a sales pitch and a go-to-market strategy, and attracting investors and keeping them. Yes, you will lose clients if the investing team performs poorly. But you will not attract them in the first place or keep them if the marketing team (also called client services or investor relations) is rubbish. Yet there is no economic recognition by hedge funds of the pecking-order revolution happening among their people.

In August 2018, the *Wall Street Journal* asked, "At hedge funds, where are the women?" The *Journal* also noted that "of the largest 50 U.S. hedge funds by assets under management, only two have women as their top investment executive, according to a *Wall Street Journal* analysis of data from researcher Absolute Return. In that same group of 50 hedge funds, half the investor relations or marketing departments have female heads or coheads."

How come the money has not followed the business model evolution and moved from the investing to the marketing team, you ask? Why, because that is where the women in hedge funds are.

CASHING OUT

And so comes the end of the golden age: visionary talents leaving the business because the industry is mature, hedge funds no longer beating the market, and fees shrinking as outsized bonuses continue to go in the opposite direction.

There is one last indicator that something is rotten in the state of Denmark. For the first decades, hedge fund founders kept all, or at least the majority, of their own money in the fund. That was the deal, the alignment of interest with investors, skin in the game. It is not only an incentive to minimize losses and maximize profit, but a way to avoid dilution. The more investors and the more assets in your hedge fund, the more you share profit with others. It was an excellent—no, a critical—idea.

This structure, however, is becoming rare. Most large hedge funds have either gone public or sold at least a minority, if not a majority ownership to a large corporation, insurance company, mutual fund, or bank. Citadel became a public company in 2015. Fortress Investment Group went public in 2007 then was bought by Japan's SoftBank Group in 2017. Oaktree Capital sold to Brookfield Asset Management in March 2019 after becoming public in 2012. These are just a few transactions in a longer string of mergers and initial public offerings, but they are emblematic of the issue. SoftBank has explicitly stated its ambition to become a $300 billion asset manager. Brookfield is Canada's largest alternative investment firm and owns assets ranging from real estate to infrastructure to renewable power.

Will a fund owned or partially owned by a multinational conglomerate have the same incentive, the same nimbleness, the same aggressiveness, and the same hunger? I think not. My prediction is that consolidation in the hedge fund industry will persist, not because it improves performance—it does not—but because large hedge fund founders want to cash out before the next Global Financial Crisis hits.

The jig is up.

MOTHER OF THE YEAR

None of this is sour grapes, I swear. Well, nothing beyond my natural cynical self. I happily retired before fifty. The way I see it, I spent half my life making money. I will spend the next half spending it. I do not miss the scrappy industry I once loved that has now exhausted itself and grown bloated beyond an ability to be dynamic. I am busy.

I read a quote from Brad Pitt recently, and I don't wish for anyone to infer that I have a lot more time to read *Vanity Fair* these days. Brad said, "When you feel like you've finally got your arms around something, then it's time to go get your arms around something else." I liked it, though I wondered if one had their arms around Brad Pitt, would one truly clock out to move them elsewhere?

All the same, the hugging concept got me thinking. I confess that I did not retire to spend more time with my family. But it is a fringe benefit. I am keenly aware of the issue of professional versus personal life balance, of course, although I find the word "balance" somewhat irksome. It suggests the even distribution of time, focus, or energy between two components in order to achieve stability or steadiness. The reality is that you cannot spend an equal amount of time between professional and personal life if you work in an office and you have a reasonable expectation to sleep at night. No one ever called me stable or steady either. Thus, there is no balance but there are choices. It sounds preachy, but the trick is to make fulfilling choices and accept the consequences.

The struggle starts early. When I announced my first maternity leave, an analyst asked me what I had planned for my "vacation." "I'm going to pop the baby out and get wasted," I said. "Maybe drugs." A friend of mine, upon announcing her pregnancy to her boss, was asked in a rather accusatory tone if it was planned. I have always wondered what the right answer was. If it was not planned, was he offering to pay for an abortion? And if it was, was it a professional betrayal?

It is simple, really. You should not be having a child on the job, but if you must have one, you must also strive for the mother of the year award. I have been on the losing end of both sides of the argument. Notice that this question of balance is rarely asked of a man, particularly on Wall Street. I do not recall reading an interview or attending a panel with George Soros, Steve Cohen, Ken Griffin, or Dan Loeb where one was asked, "Tell me, Dan, how do you find the time for parent-teacher conferences, what with the public board battle against Campbell Soup and all? How do you weigh the end-of-school ballet and coercing United Technologies into splitting the business?" Yet how to balance one's professional and personal life was a question asked on every panel on which I ever spoke, including the loosely related topic "EETC: Are Enhanced Features Worth a Yield Discount?"

For my fellow working women out there who feel dreadfully guilty about not baking cookies for fundraising, never being a class delegate, missing the school play, not helping in the library, needing a name tag to mingle at the school social, confusing the headmaster with the security guard, taking a minute to remember your children's class grades (give me a break, it's a different system in France), you are not alone. Except I do not feel guilty.

At one parent-teacher conference (these I tried not to miss) I sat proudly, on time, name tag affixed, cell phone off, ready to gravely debate the advantages of visual aid versus formative assessments while teaching math in primary school when a mother leaned over and whispered to me, "What are you doing here?"

"What do you mean," I said, outraged, "I am here to further my son's education. What are *you* doing here?"

"You're in the wrong place," she said, "Your kid is in the other class."

Quietly thanking her, I took myself on a walk of shame of sorts, across the entire room and into the other class, where my husband was already in position. "Wrong classroom?" he smirked. Say, who ended up helping with math homework in the end? And let's not argue, because it would be petty, that we were in Paris by then and that the spatial geometry questions were, well, in French.

It does not follow that I am not a good parent because I could not and did not want to be a stay-at-home mother. I bet you can be a truly lousy parent if you are a full-time mother who believes that your life revolves around your children and nothing else appeals or makes you curious, excited, joyful, and personally fulfilled. Your children will leave, you see. That is a fact, and that's a good thing, so you'd better have a life on your own. I do not think children are particularly well served by helicopter or snowplow parents who obsess over every boo-boo, resolve every conflict, and flatten out every hurdle. It is a lack of respect, a mistrust as it were, rooted in the conviction that the child cannot face life with the inevitable difficulties that ensue on his own. Here's an idea: your child is not an extension of you.

A DAY WITHOUT WOMEN

I am proud of my gender. In case it has not been clear thus far, I can prove it.

A short few months before leaving Canyon, on March 8, 2017, International Women's Day, a U.S.-wide strike was planned to oppose the policies of the Trump administration. They called it the Day Without a Woman protest, and organizers encouraged women to show solidarity by wearing red, refraining from spending money, and not going to work.

Now, men on Wall Street must have had a good laugh at the last part. Every day is pretty much International Women's Day by that standard. I had to show up to work, but I did wear red head to toe, a sort of Gucci Bordeaux because it suits my skin tone. Fashion need not be subordinated to a political statement, no matter how just. Besides, I had a meeting with Goldman Sachs and lipstick red is a smidge bearish.

I was making myself an espresso in the kitchen. Our office had not one, but two kitchens. The one nearest my office was adjacent to the two non-gender-specific bathrooms designated for the analyst pool and the trading floor. Because of this dual destination, it was a mass transit area. While waiting for my beans to grind, I reflected upon how enthusiastically junior hedge fund analysts snarf free food—*any* free food. It cannot be hunger for folks whose bonuses are a million dollars or more. It is an addiction. Free food is a high. It's a win. For years, before banking regulations restrained gifts to hedge funds, December marked the beginning of gargantuan amounts of edible presents sent by our vendors (lawyers, brokers, advisors, accountants, software providers), each more improbable than the next. There was the colossal ten gallons of popcorn packaged in a festive red tin bucket, with three flavors: natural, caramel, and cheese. One year, we got three of them from three different banks, which about tells you how sophisticated a palate and imaginative a mind these fellows have.

The mystifying fact is that it was all eaten in a day. Sometimes within an hour. No matter what it was, a smorgasbord of fruit shaped like flowers—or was it flowers shaped like fruit?—onion spread, Cheese Whiz, bacon cookies, tonic water crackers, peanut brittle, and pickle-flavored jerky, among other products that my French background had blissfully kept me a virgin of. My all-time favorite was a giant fifty-inch chocolate Eiffel Tower. It stood on its own! You could break it apart and eat the top floor! How I would cherish the thought that someone on Wall Street wished to impress me and flatter my patriotism with that true miracle of gastronomy. Alas, it was the ritual present of a French bank. My own people.

As I recall that morning of International Women's Day, a partner came into the kitchen holding a bag of sliced bread. Since when does a multimillionaire hedge fund manager eat carbs? you chortle. Wait. That is not even the story. As it turns out, the frozen gluten-free millet-chia bread, something between bird feed and slave food in Mesopotamia, needed a whiff of reheating. The partner stopped in front of the toaster looking puzzled, even mildly alarmed.

"Let's see here. How does this work? Dominique, how do I do this?"

I checked that my hearing was right and said inquisitively "Do you mean how to toast your bread?"

"Yes. How does it work? What do I do?"

I obliged. Like a mime, because I could not manhandle his bread, could I? I demonstrated with great drama and hand gesture amplitude that one puts the slice into the slot, here, and presses the toast button thusly. I hate to flatter myself, but I do believe I found the right tone of female support, invoking the ideal of Athena, goddess of protection, encouraging him along the way "Exactly. Right. Steady."

"I see. I got it!" he said.

"Nicely done," I replied.

A Day Without a Woman is a day without toast.

That was that. I had made my mark on Wall Street.

ACKNOWLEDGMENTS

I would like to acknowledge my wonderful writing coach, Stuart Horwitz. I hope to call him a friend, now that this is all behind us. Many thanks to my agent, Leslie York, for believing in the project and moving the proposal forward (blame her for my lousy attempt to build a Twitter following.) There would be no story to tell without Josh Friedman and Mitch Julis—my gratitude for a wonderful career and hilarious memories. I wish my mother could have read the book; my beloved father was one of the first readers. Finally, thank you Juan, my knight and my dragon; it's nice to be liked, if you know what I mean.

ENDNOTES

1 Brad M. Barber and Terrance Odean, "Boys Will Be Boys: Gender, Overconfidence, and Common Stock Investment," *The Quarterly Journal of Economics*, February 2001, https://academic.oup.com/qje/article-abstract/116/1/261/1939000?redirectedFrom=fulltext

2 Pauline R. Clance and Suzanne A. Imes, "The Impostor Phenomenon in High Achieving Women: Dynamics and Therapeutic Intervention," *Psychotherapy Theory, Research and Practice*, Fall 1978, https://psycnet.apa.org/record/1979-26502-001

3 Stacey Chin, Alexis Krivkovich, and Marie-Claude Nadeau, "Constraints into preference: Gender, status and emerging career aspirations," Sept. 6, 2018, https://www.mckinsey.com/industries/financial-services/our-insights/closing-the-gap-leadership-perspectives-on-promoting-women-in-financial-services

4 Amy J. C. Cuddy, Matthew Kohut, and John Netfinger, "Connect, Then Lead," *Harvard Business Review*, July-August 2013, https://hbr.org/2013/07/connect-then-lead

5 Rajesh K. Aggarwal and Nicole M. Boyson, "The Performance of Female Hedge Fund Managers," *Review of Financial Economics*, April 2016, https://www.sciencedirect.com/science/article/abs/pii/S1058330016000148

6 Robin Furneaux, *The Amazon: The Story of a Great River*, New York: G. P. Putnam's Sons, 1967.

7 Sheen S. Levine, Evan P. Apfelbaum, Mark Bernard, Valerie L. Bartelt, Edward J. Zajac, and David Stark, "Ethnic Diversity Deflates Price Bubbles," Proceedings of the National Academy of Sciences of the United States of America, Nov. 16, 2014, https://www.pnas.org/content/111/52/18524

8 Krista L. Nelson, Danielle N. Newman, Janelle R. McDanial, and Walter C. Buboltz, "Gender Differences in Fear of Failures amongst Engineering Students," *International Journal of Humanities and Social Science*,

August 2013, http://www.ijhssnet.com/journals/Vol_3_No_16_Special_Issue_August_2013/2.pdf

9 Aggarwal and Boyson.

10 Victoria L. Brescoll, Erica Dawson and Eric Luis Uhlmann, "Hard Won and Easily Lost: The Fragile Status of Leaders in Gender-Stereotype-Incongruent Occupations," *Psychological Science*, November 2010, https://www.jstor.org/stable/41062426?seq=1

11 Mark L. Egan, Gregor Matvos, and Amit Seru, "When Harry Fired Sally: The Double Standard in Punishing Misconduct," National Bureau of Economic Research, March 2017, https://www.nber.org/papers/w23242